"Susan captures the messy and marvelous of being in God's family and used for kingdom purposes. Everywhere, I saw myself and my Savior. This book is a gift and a tool, scripture-filled and infused with quotes and wisdom from Augustine to Ida B. Wells. Prepare to be challenged and strengthened in your faith!"

Ronjanett Taylor, Former At-Large Advisor for Diversity, PCA Women's Ministry

"The five women of Matthew tell our story and our struggles of feeling alone, unseen, forsaken, voiceless, disenfranchised, and not enough by giving words to ours. Susan winsomely guides us to see how our stories matter to Christ because these five women mattered to Him."

Alice Kim, Therapist at Emmaus Counseling and Consulting Services, LLC

"I heartily endorse Susan Tyner's *What's SHE Doing Here?* It is an outstanding Bible study resource on a critical gospel topic deeply rooted in the Bible with accessibility and adaptability across a wide range of contexts. Susan reflects her own deep biblical formation in the gospel of grace as she welcomes and engages all kinds of women across various life callings, circumstances, and diverse backgrounds. This is a wonderful new gospel resource for the church!"

Dr. Mark L. Dalbey, President, and Professor of Applied Theology at Covenant Seminary

"The opening pages of Matthew's gospel loudly proclaim that Jesus came to save the lost, the messy, and the broken. If that news is as good for you as it is for me, then this Bible study is for you. Susan Tyner shows us how God not only wove His story of salvation together with a prostitute, a foreigner, a teen mom, and other "messy women," she shows us how He is also weaving your story and mine into His today. What a glorious Savior we have!"

Courtney Doctor, Coordinator of Women's Initiatives, The Gospel Coalition and author of *From Garden to Glory: A Bible Study on the Bible's Story* and *Steadfast; A Devotional Bible Study on the Book of James* and co-author of *Remember Your Joy: A Bible Study of Salvation Stories in the Old Testament*

"*What's SHE Doing Here?* is an exploration of the depths of God's unconditional love. Susan Tyner provides an easy-to-use study that encourages you to see your story, with all of its messiness, in the light of God's bigger story of redemption. Susan enables you to see the women in "old Bible stories" as people you can identify with. More importantly, she leads you to see the God who meets people at the point of their deep need and insecurity. God doesn't hide messy people or hide from them; He highlights them. This study will encourage you even as it equips you to search Scripture for truth."

Dr. Stephen T. Estock, Coordinator, PCA Discipleship Ministries (CDM)

"Susan Tyner's love for and knowledge of God's Word, combined with her wisdom, wit, and winsomeness, make this a compelling and delightful study. She brings us face-to-face with sisters from Scripture who show us God's covenant love and loyalty to His people."

Susan Hunt, Former Coordinator for Women's Ministries (PCA) and author of many books for women and children including, *Aging with Grace*.

"Ever felt like an outsider because of your story? Susan winsomely invites the outsider in by introducing us to five less-than-perfect women in the family of Jesus. She reminds us that their stories and ours are part of a grand story the Lord is writing with each bump, turn, and plot twist. Only read this book if you want to be encouraged and welcomed into the fellowship of the imperfect!"

Vanessa K. Hawkins, Director of Women's Ministry at First Presbyterian Church, Augusta, GA, and Diversity Advisor for PCA Women's Ministry

"Most women desire a friend with whom to share the real-deal of life, be encouraged in Christ, and enjoy a deep laugh. Susan Tyner is that kind of friend, and this rich study does all of the above! If you're a messy woman needy of grace, grab a friend and read this book together."

Ellen Mary Dykas, Women's Ministry Coordinator, Harvest USA, and author of *Toxic Relationships: Taking Refuge in Christ*, and *Sexual Faithfulness: Gospel-infused, Practical Discipleship for Women*

"Ever wonder about some of the women in Jesus's genealogy? They aren't your typical cleaned-up, high achieving, have-their-act-together kind of women. *What's SHE Doing Here?* is a gospel-laced study which traces God's covenant-keeping faithfulness in His story of redemption, including the lives of messy, brokenhearted, and empty-handed women. Each of these women in Jesus's genealogy is a testimony of God's grace—as are we! Get this study and rejoice in God's transforming work in the lives of the messy."

Christina Fox, counselor, retreat speaker, PCA Women's Ministry Regional Advisor to the Southeast, author of several books, including *A Holy Fear: Trading Lesser Fears for the Fear of the Lord*

"Susan Tyner asks the question many of us in the church have asked, 'What's she doing here?' or, more personally, 'What am I doing here?' Our sin and shame often keep us from resting in the person and work of Jesus Christ, the One to whom all Scripture points. In this delightful study of the five unlikely women in Jesus's genealogy, your mind will be sharpened, your heart warmed, and your hands prepared to reach out, by God's grace, to those around you with the compassion and love of Christ."

Sarah Ivill, Bible teacher and author of *The Covenantal Life: Appreciating the Beauty of Theology and Community*

"*What's SHE Doing Here? The Messy Women in Jesus's Genealogy* is a journey through God's redemptive story to rescue, deliver, and adopt a messy people. Throughout this study, Susan Tyner graciously introduces readers to the unlikely mamas in Jesus's genealogy, showing women that they are not unique, strange, or alone in the messiness of life on earth. With biblical teaching and relatable stories, the gospel shines brightly through Susan's words—Jesus loves the messy. As members of God's covenant family, we should imitate the love of our Big Brother Jesus—loving those who are lovely to Him."

Rachel Ann Craddock, speaker, author of *Slowly Unraveled: Changed from the Inside Out*, and CDM's Regional Advisor to Women's Ministries in Mid America

"If you've ever felt out of place in the kingdom of God or 'disqualified' because of your past sins and mistakes, then Susan Tyner has a message for you in this book. On every page, she reminds us that we're all a mess without Jesus! But Jesus doesn't just put up with us—He welcomes us to His Father's table. He has set a place just for you. Susan reminds us that in the kingdom of God, messy women are wanted because God does His greatest work of redemption through sinful, broken people. Listen to Susan's word of hope for us: '[God] continues to use women like us in His salvation plan for the world.' You belong here, you are welcome here, and Jesus longs to enfold you into His great story of redemption. He owned these five messy women as His mamas, and He longs to own you as His little sister. Thank you, Susan, for this beautiful and hopeful study!"

Abby Hutto, Director of Spiritual Formation at Story Presbyterian Church, Westerville, Ohio, and author of *God For Us: Discovering the Father through the Life of the Son*.

"This study of the women in Jesus's genealogy is just fantastic. It does not ask too much, nor too little, of its readers as they study the lives of these women. This study does not shy away from difficult questions about God and about the lives of these women. The material is deep and challenging yet easy to understand. This guide is bound to lead you to a deeper knowledge of who God is and why He chose these particular women to be in the lineage of Christ. The Leader's Guide in the Appendix completes the book as it makes leading a small group very doable and clear. I look forward to using this book with our PCPC women!"

Kari Stainback, Director of Women's Ministries Park Cities Presbyterian Church, Dallas, TX

"Matthew, a social outcast prior to being a disciple, understood first-hand Jesus's love and compassion for those suffering and in need. While leading us through a study of the suffering matriarchs of Jesus's family, Susan Tyner reminds us that Jesus came not for the perfect but to bring justice and redemption to the weary, marginalized, and suffering."

Becky Kiern, Speaker and author of *Our Light and Life: Identity in the Claims of Christ*

What's SHE Doing Here?
THE MESSY WOMEN IN JESUS'S GENEALOGY

Susan Tyner

© 2021 Susan Tyner
Cover Art: Susan Woodard Kelly

Published by:
Committee on Discipleship Ministries
1700 North Brown Road, Suite 102
Lawrenceville, Georgia 30043
Bookstore: 1-800-283-1357
www.pcacdm.org/bookstore

All rights reserved. No part of this book may be reproduced, stored in a retrieval system, or transmitted in any form or by any means—electronically, mechanical, photocopy, recording, or otherwise—except as expressly allowed herein or for brief quotations for the purpose of review or comment, without the prior permission of the publisher, Committee on Discipleship Ministries, at the above address.

The Holy Bible, English Standard Version™ Copyright © 2000; 2001; 2016 by Crossway Bibles, A Division of Good News Publishers, 1300 Crescent Street, Wheaton, Illinois 60187, USA. All Rights Reserved.

This edition published by arrangement with Crossway Bibles, a Division of Good News Publishers. The Holy Bible, English Standard Version™ is adapted from the Revised Standard Version of the Bible, copyright Division of Christian Education of the National Council of Churches of Christ in the USA. All Rights Reserved.

Although many publishers do not capitalize terms, and particularly pronouns, which refer to the Trinity, in this study CDM publications has capitalized those elements for clarity of reference.

ISBN: 978-1-944964-57-3

Visit the web site www.pcacdm.org/messy for video content and more.

For Mama who showed me how to thread the covenant pearls and Daddy who showed me how to live like the Bible is true.

"Visit many good books, but live in the Bible."
—Charles Spurgeon

What's SHE Doing Here?
THE MESSY WOMEN IN JESUS'S GENEALOGY

How to Use This Study 9

The Not So Fabulous Five 17

God's Story 27

The Desperate Daughter-in-Law 39

The Career Prostitute 53

The Ultimate Outsider 67

From Outsider to Ultimate Insider 79

The Queen of Messy 95

The Unwed Teen Mother 111

Magnificat! 125

In Closing 139

Appendix
Leader's Guide for Small Group Discussion 143
Prayer Request Charts 145
Suggested Discussion Questions 157

How to Use This Study

In years of teaching Bible studies, my favorite question I've ever been asked is, "Can I come to your study even if I don't have a Bible?" The answer? "Yes! And, by the way, I've got an extra Bible I'd love to give you." As you begin *What's SHE Doing Here?* I hope you will buy a Bible, dust off a Bible, or grab your Bible off your bedside table and join us as we learn about God's character and Jesus's "messy mamas." And since many women like to travel light or use a Bible app, the primary passages for each chapter are given in the chart on page 14.

What's SHE Doing Here? is written for individual or small group use. You can watch the videos supplied by CDM (www.pcacdm.org/messy), or your local church may want a "live" teacher while using this book to prompt study beforehand and discussion after the lectures. I've found that I learn better when I learn alongside someone else. A term we will discuss in the pages ahead is covenant. It is shorthand in the Bible for how God relates to His people. The *covenant community* is your spiritual family. One of the ways women grow in their faith is to spend time with other women who love God. Studying God's Word with other believers not only increases your wisdom for living, but also cultivates more relationship ties as no one can do life alone. So, identify a nearby co-worker, a new girl at school, or another mom in the neighborhood and ask her if she'd like to meet once a week to discuss this book and the Bible passages included. Or gather a group of friends in your dorm or church. Consider intentionally including women who may not be invited to many Bible studies.

Hearing the Bible taught and then discussing implications of His Word for our lives is a great way to learn. If you are leading a small group discussion, congrats on being brave! Every excuse from "I don't know my Bible well enough" to "I don't have time to prepare" keeps smart, capable, and caring women from leading other women through the Bible.

If you are leading a church or community Bible study, suggestions for doing so are in the back (p. 143). These tips include praying to understand the passages, sharing how those scriptures impact your daily living, and creating accountability for applying God's Word to your season of life. Also included in the back (p. 145) is space to keep up with prayer requests, whether they are your own or requests from your group members.

If you are part of a group or if you are studying alone, find a space to pray, asking God's Spirit to help you understand what you are reading in His Word, the Bible. Then, read a chapter, answering the questions along the way. Consider keeping a journal as you have thoughts or questions for further study. If you want to memorize scripture as part of this study, suggested passages are included as well as downloadable pages to print on the website (www.pcacdm.org/messy).

Each chapter of this study is broken into three sections: Her Story, God's Story, and Your Story. The study is written for women who want to open their Bibles yet cannot spend hours each week on a Bible study. Working through each chapter should take no longer than two hours per week, including the video lesson or podcast (www.pcacdm.org/messy). You may take just a few minutes each day to work through one section of a chapter, or she may take on all three sections in one sitting. It is up to you! Room is provided in each chapter for journaling thoughts, jotting down questions, or just writing out prayers as God's Word moves you. If your interest is piqued and you want to learn more about God's story, check out the resources for further study in the back of the book.

Her Story

Each woman we read about was a real person. She had to find something to wear every morning, and she crashed into bed at the end of her long day. God saw her story from start to finish (Ps. 139:16), and He guided her, protected her, provided for her, and accomplished His plans for her life (Jer. 1:5). He knew how many hairs she brushed everyday (Matt. 10:30).

God's Story

Although God is intimately involved in His daughters' lives, He is also weaving their stories into His Big story. He takes all the pearls of their stories and other Bible stories and strings them together into a beautiful necklace. Some call this pearl necklace His covenant with His people; the plot of His Big Story is to make us His special people (1 Peter 2:9). As a God who pursues, He is also a God who orchestrates a story of salvation for many. Nothing skews His plotline, not even our stories of failure and weakness (Isa. 14:27).

God used our study's five ordinary women to accomplish an extraordinary redemption of His creation and His people. And, throughout the chapters you will see what I like to call Bible Lagniappe. Growing up in Mississippi, I often heard the term *lagniappe*, "a little something extra." Look out for the Bible Lagniappe sprinkled throughout the study to connect the dots of each woman's story to the bigger story of the Bible.

Your Story

God continues to string pearls on His beautiful necklace of redemption. Your life is one of His pearls. From stay-at-home moms to CEOs, from bus drivers to Air Force pilots, women's stories vary, and so does the way God uses their gifts, experiences, and obedience to execute His plans for our world. You may feel like your story is mundane, the same laundry day after day. Perhaps you are lonely when you see couples dine out as you eat in a booth alone. You may feel isolated among friends based on your background or even the color of your skin. You may even want to push back on the term "messy." Whether you are insecure or proud about the way you are living your life, God's story supersedes yours (Isa. 55:8-9). While this truth can be jarring in a culture that emphasizes our individuality and independence, it can also bring comfort—there is meaning in and beyond the circumstances of our stories (Rom. 8:28).

I hope you enjoy knowing the five women of Matthew 1. More importantly, I want you to know their God as your own and to learn more about God's Big Story as you study theirs. And as you do, see how their God of justice, mercy, and love meets you in the personal details of life while saving an entire world. One messy story at a time.

Let's Get Started

Here is an idea of what to do, when ...

- Pray for wisdom to understand God's Word you will be reading.
- Read a chapter of *What's SHE Doing Here?* and work through the questions. In the margins, jot down questions or new truths you may want to bring up to your small group.
- Watch the video or listen to the podcast (www.pcacdm.org/messy), whether individually or as a group.
- Attend your small group discussion (or flip through those questions on your own). Practice memory work if that is a personal or group goal.
- Close in individual prayer or share prayer requests with your group. Pray for those needs between small group meetings.

Beyond the Study

Covenant Community

Making friends through Bible study can present further opportunities for accountability and encouragement. Consider ways to build relationships with the women in your group outside your regular meetings.

#HerVoice

Depending on how much time you have for small group discussion, take turns asking individual women to come prepared to share a five-minute story from their lives and how it applies to what you are learning in this study. Or if that is too scary, consider asking a woman to come prepared to answer the ice breaker question that kicks off the group's discussion that day.

Be on the Lookout

As leaders we must always be looking for the next woman to replace us. As you listen to discussion, be sensitive to those who exhibit potential to lead the next group, perhaps to be a teacher herself, or to organize a conference or mercy ministry for your church. I would never have started teaching if not for my teacher giving me a fifteen-minute slot to "practice teach" at my Bible study and her words of "Well done!" afterwards.

End Together

Add a closing week to your Bible study schedule for all the groups to meet together to share ways this study impacted their view of other women, themselves, or God.

Throw A Party!

Every good thing has to end, but you can also end in a celebratory way. God's people should throw the best parties because our God made all good things. This is a great time to include women who are good at organizing events or are gifted in hospitality or who know how to set a festive table. Celebrate what you've learned as a group and the new women you have met during this season.

Think Outside the Box

This study does not have to stick to the schedule given in the table of contents. Go to our webpage (www.pcacdm.org/messy) for helpful tools and a schedule template to plan a study tailor-made to your women's schedules and needs. Be creative! Find a group of women and adapt the study schedule to work best with theirs. Perhaps your group cannot meet weekly, so you take a chapter each month and stretch it over the fall or spring. Consider asking an older woman and a friend to open their homes (and maybe an apartment complex's pool) and co-lead a group of college girls for a summer study. Or, maybe you just include this *What's SHE Doing Here?* as a book-of-the-month reading for your neighborhood book club. For women who cannot make it to a group for various reasons, offer a virtual study including options for Zoom small groups. Check out www.pcacdm.org/messy for online resources.

Take Down Barriers

Ask your church to fund childcare if it is a moms' group. Consider meeting at a restaurant near your office complex so women can conveniently stop by for Bible study and dinner on the way home from work. If your group loves to exercise, plan a post-walk Bible study meeting in your sweatiest clothes, water bottles in tow. You can even discuss the questions as you walk!

Date	Lesson	Read Chapter	Primary Passages	Memory Work
	The Not So Fabulous Five	1	Matt. 1:1-17 Phil. 2:6-7	2 Cor. 5:17
	God's Story	2	Gen. 1-3 Rev. 21	Eph. 2:8-9
	The Desperate Daughter-in-Law	3	Gen. 38	Ps. 20:7
	The Career Prostitute	4	Joshua 2	John 14:6
	The Ultimate Outsider	5	The Book of Ruth	Ps. 91:14
	From Outsider to Ultimate Insider	6	The Book of Ruth	Ps. 62:11-12a
	The Queen of Messy	7	2 Sam. 11-12	Ps. 51:10
	The Unwed Teenage Mother	8	Luke 1:1-38	Prov. 3:5
	Magnificat!	9	Luke 1:46-55	Rom. 8:31-32

Introduction

When I was little, I remember waiting in the doctor's office. I lived in a small Mississippi farming community, and the office was simple but personal. On the wall was a large, framed portrait of Ruth, one of the women we will consider in this study. She looked so beautiful—serene, brunette, in pink Middle Eastern dress, gently cradling a bunch of barley. I guess it made me calm. After all, I was a brunette, too, and I wanted to be calm—especially waiting for a possible injection. I wanted to be attractive like the Ruth in the painting, waiting on my Boaz to marry me so I could quit working in a hot barley field.

If the real Ruth, the one from the Bible, saw that office print, she would laugh! A young widow and recent immigrant to Bethlehem, Ruth is not even described as pretty. She lived with a grouchy mother-in-law and had to work in a dangerous field. That soft, flowing, Middle Eastern dress was probably stained with dust, smelling like a locker room.

Romanticized portraits of biblical women do not really offer much to women today. Not only are they sanitized accounts of who these women really were, but they put unrealistic expectations on us and lead us away from the truths God teaches us with their stories. God's purpose in our lives is not for us to be in that kind of framed print, looking all perfect and peaceful. The messiness of our lives reveals our need for the type of Savior we've been offered. God doesn't save women to Himself so they can hang on a wall. He saves them so they can sit at His table.

In this study we will look at the lives of the five women included in Jesus's genealogy in Matthew 1. I hope we will have a better understanding of why God included these particular women in His family record, how He worked in their lives, and how He does the same in ours. In each chapter we will look at their stories, how their stories intersect with God's Big Story, and how the passages can affect our stories today. The chapters are broken up into three days of study and soul-searching, or you can work through the whole chapter in one sitting. The questions are meant for individual study or small group discussion.

1
The Not-So-Fabulous Five

The other night I went to bed feeling messy. Icky. Unsettled.

The memory of a conversation with a friend about another friend weighed on my mind. What if my words were taken out of context? What if others found out what I had said? Was I a gossip hidden in "good girl" clothes?

Many women go to bed unsettled for worse reasons than a less-than-kind water-cooler conversation. Maybe stinging words from a co-worker last year still echo in your mind. Perhaps sleeping in a loveless marriage weighs you down. The chaos of what we flip through on a daily basis on social media, TV, and on the car radio—a constant barrage of the messy world we live in—creates a craving for order, dependability, and peace.

> Q. 16: What is sin?
>
> A: Sin is rejecting or ignoring God in the world he created, rebelling against him by living without reference to him, not being or doing what he requires in his law—resulting in our death and the disintegration of all creation.[1]

What does messy mean to you? According to the Merriam-Webster Dictionary, *messy* is defined as "marked by confusion or untidy; lacking neatness or precision and even extremely unpleasant or trying."[2] Whether due to others' sins, the normal brokenness of life, or just our own bad choices, our lives can look messy, and messy is an overwhelming place to be. This study hopes to show how the perfect and holy God sent a Savior who identifies with a messy people and gives us hope.

> "God redeems us through and in His messy grace. It's messy because God doesn't free us from disappointment and struggle and suffering, He doesn't free us as if though all our sins are going to go away magically, but His grace does deliver life, hope and mercy. There is true and real change in and through the grace that God brings when He meets us in that place of messy brokenness."
> —Tom Gibbs[3]

Day One: Her Story

Read Matthew 1:1-17.

1. List the five women included in Matthew's genealogy:

2. This is the only gospel genealogy that includes women. Why do you think Matthew's version does so?

Why these five women? Why not Sarah, the wife of Abraham? Leah, mother of Israel's kings? Why did Matthew include women who experienced the messiness of neglect, abuse, poverty, and unexpected life changes? Most of us introduce our families with the remarkable members—those who thrive or are at least socially acceptable. We want to be associated

> "God answers the mess of life with one word: Grace."
> —Max Lucado[4]

The Not-So-Fabulous Five

with the good people in our families and keep the others hidden. But Jesus, the only person who ever got to choose His family, doesn't hide the messes. He highlights them for all to see. He unashamedly says they're His.

The scripture references for the stories we know of these five women can be found in the chart that follows. Over this week's lesson, pick one or two of the passages to read each day and become acquainted with the women Matthew introduces. As you meet each woman in our study, try to put yourself in her shoes. How did it feel to be where she was? What would that look like today? We'll connect the dots to other stories God tells throughout Scripture and see how they're all pieces of His Story.

Through looking at the lives of these five ladies, we hope to get a better look at God and how He interacts with His people.

> "This act of helping 'different' women move from living with heads down to up is not new to us. God has exemplified it for us repeatedly in his Word."
>
> —Soojin Park[5]

3. Over the next few days, read about our five women. Today, read the passages from Genesis and Joshua and fill in the chart below.

Her Name	Her Story	Her Messy Circumstances	
Tamar	Gen. 38	Canaanite woman, first two husbands were wicked, father in law pushed her away, prostituted herself	Shamed to death
Rahab	Josh. 2, 6:22-25	Prostitute, lies (to being brave)	
Ruth	Book of Ruth	Husband died, foreigner, left family, life of sacrifice.	
Bathsheba	2 Sam. 11:1-12:25	Betrayed husband with king, husband got killed by king. Son dies	
Mary	Luke 1:26-2:52	Virgin birth of Jesus (teenager). fleeing, and circumstance of birth.	

Day Two: God's Story

1. Today, read the book of Ruth and fill in the corresponding information in the previous chart.

How can a holy God—a perfect God—and a messy people co-exist? Matthew's introduction of the much-anticipated Messiah, including a laundry list of messed-up men and women, gives us a clue. Christ's association with this litany of sinners shows exactly what kind of Messiah He is: a Savior who will get down in the mess alongside us. When my children were little and one of my kids got really dirty—maybe she vomited, or he had a really messy diaper—I had to get dirty in order to get them clean, right? As they cried and needed my help, I had to scoop them up, experiencing the stink too.

2. Read Philippians 2:6-7 (NIV). Circle or underline the words that stand out to you.

> Who, being in very nature God, did not consider equality with God something to be used to his own advantage; rather, he made himself nothing by taking the very nature of a servant, being made in human likeness.

Pray: Help me shop/read and understand your word!

A righteous Jesus loved us enough to scoop us up. He put Himself in a place to feel fatigue, to feel bullied, to even feel death to save us from our messy choices, messy world, and messy hearts. He could not—nor did He want to—save us from a comfortable distance. Our salvation is about relationship with Him, so the means of that salvation will include relationship, even with women as messy as we are. We will look in next week's lesson at how our individual stories fit in with God's overall story of salvation for our messy world, as well as for the women like us in it.

The Not-So-Fabulous Five

3. How can Jesus's humility in getting messy with us impact how we view others' messiness?

   We are not better than them nor are they better than us. We are all messy and need Jesus - the only spotless one.
   It is so loving when someone gets messy for us to help us.

4. When has your messiness been useful as you comfort another in hers?

   It shows that she is not special and we all are messy. To be okay not being okay all the time + and use this to help / minister to others.

5. How does the truth of Philippians 2:6-7 help you accept God's forgiveness?

   Hebr. 4:14-16. God sympathize with our weakness since God took on human likeness. So he knows and is loving and can forgive.
   Jesus was sent to save us. God's wrath is his righteousness and he is just. And with Jesus his son he saves us! What a sacrifice!!
   How loving. If you think you are not worthy of forgiveness you put yourself above him.

Day Three: Your Story

1. Complete the chart from Day One, reading the passages from 2 Samuel and Luke.

2. What patterns do you see emerging in these women's lives?

   - *Poverty (Mary + Ruth were poor + Rahab)*
   - *God is at the center of the story*
   - *They had faith in the god of Israel? (except Ruth) despite suffering*
   - *all suffered*
   - *Losses (suffering)*
   - *Jesus → story's about redemption*

   > Blessed be the God and Father of our Lord Jesus Christ, the Father of mercies and God of all comfort, who comforts us in all our affliction, so that we may be able to comfort those who are in any affliction, with the comfort with which we ourselves are comforted by God (2 Cor. 1:3-4).

3. How did God treat them?
   He did not judge them like man would. Treat them with kindness & grace & mercy.

4. Based on your reading throughout the week, choose one woman from our study whose story resonates most with yours:
   a. How is your story similar to hers?

   b. How is it different?

5. Name some ways you have seen God work in your story as He worked in hers.
   My circumstances change, God's don't. His mercy stays.

> "We must realize that Christianity is the easiest religion in the world, because it is the only religion in which God the Father and Christ and the Holy Spirit do everything."
> —Francis Schaeffer[6]

You may scan these women's stories and see a narrative that reminds you of a personal time of brokenness, or you may relate to the idea of just being messy in a messy world. On the other hand, you may feel like you have it all together and things are not very messy at all. Wherever you find yourself, let's seek to more fully know the love of Jesus through this study. These five ladies can teach us that God not only uses our messes in His plan of redemption, but He calls us family along the way. He identifies with us and leads us to find our identities in Him.

Lord, I'm Willing[7]

Lord, it's more than I'll ever understand,
How I am preserved by Thy hand.
But then there's only two things required of me:
To be faithful (because I've been set free)
And to be willing to be used by Thee.
So Lord I come willing to be used by Thee.

Lord, I am willing.
Lord, I am willing your will and way to see
Lord, I am willing. Lord, I am willing.
Lord, I am willing to be used by Thee.

Though sometimes I don't feel worthy,
consecrate me. I'm saved, I'm not the same.
Though the world may under-rate me,
dedicate me so I'll be wholly changed.

Lord, I am willing. Here I stand.
Lord, I am willing. Take my hand
and keep me by thy grace,
so I can run this race.

Bible Lagniappe
God Wants to Be at Home with Us

Have you ever noticed, at Christmas, songs call Jesus by the name Emmanuel? This means "God with us." But God was calling His Son Emmanuel long before Jesus was born in a manger (Isa. 7:14). God was also living among His people in a tent during Moses's leadership (Lev. 26:11-12). He is not only with His people as a whole, but with His individual sons and daughters in their scariest places as He told Joshua before battle (Josh. 1:9) and as David sang when he repented of serious sins (Ps. 51:11-12).

 **Memory Verse**

Therefore, if anyone is in Christ, he is a new creation. The old has passed away; behold, the new has come (2 Cor. 5:17).

---

[1] The Gospel Coalition, *New City Catechism for Kids* (Wheaton, IL: Crossway, 2018), 46-47.

[2] https://www.merriam-webster.com/dictionary/messy.

[3] Tom Gibbs, "Messy Grace" (Redeemer Presbyterian Church, San Antonio: Sermon released November 22. 2015), https://www.redeemersa.org/resources/multimedia/details?id=708273.

[4] Max Lucado, "God's Answer for the Mess of Life," *Words of Hope and Help* (blog), July 2, 2019, https://maxlucado.com/listen/gods-answer-for-the-mess-of-life.

[5] Soojin Park, "Asian American Sisters, God Lifts Your Heads High," *The Gospel Coalition* (blog), March 25, 2021, https://www.thegospelcoalition.org/article/asian-americans-lift-heads.

[6] Francis Schaeffer, "The God Who Is There" in *The Francis A. Schaeffer Trilogy: The Three Essential Books in One Volume* (Wheaton, IL: Crossway, 1990), 182-183.

[7] Genna Rae McNeil, "Lord I'm Willing" in *Conversations with God: Two Centuries of Prayers by African Americans*, edited by James Melvin Washington (New York, NY: HarperCollins Publishers, Inc., 1994), 256.

Notes

2
God's Story

Eve didn't do us any favors. She pulled the first string that unraveled the fairytale Eden (Gen. 1&2) when she fell for the words of the snake and ignored God's simple command not to eat of the Tree (Gen. 3:1-6). Grabbing that piece of fruit along with a chance at power, Eve created The Big Mess—a mess we continue to live in today.

God made His world to be enjoyed, and His favorite part was Adam and Eve. After putting them into His garden, He summed up His feelings by stamping "very good" on it all (2:31). However, this amazing world was not a fancy snow globe to sit on God's shelf and look pretty. He loved to live alongside Adam and Eve in this paradise. He had a habit of joining them in the "cool of the day" (Gen. 3:8). But one day He came to walk and found no one. "Where are you?" God asked (Gen. 3:9). Adam and Eve shrank back, hovering behind their fig leaves, ashamed. The relationship was broken. Creation's moaning had begun (Rom. 8:22).

Adam and Eve's sin did not catch God off-guard, though. He already had a plan. He did not smash the snow globe and start over with a new creation. Instead, God began to take care of this mess, even though it would cost Him. He would have to get messy Himself to rescue His people.

Day One: Their Stories

A good rescue begins with a plan. In this case the plan is called a "covenant of grace." The word *covenant* is a formal, legal word, but it means agreement. This agreement is how God put into action saving you and me, but this covenant alone would not take away the judgment our sins deserve. Somebody would still have to pay that price tag, and that Somebody would be Jesus. (See notes on the Big Story of the Bible Timeline as reference.)

"A covenant is a bond in blood sovereignly administered."
—O. Palmer Robertson[1]

The five women we are studying lived in the light of Eve's choice, as well as in the midst of God's rescue of His people and His world. After all, God wanted to enjoy Adam and Eve, but now intimacy was impossible due to their rebellious choice. The ones who walked with God were now His enemies. Like Eve, and like the five women in our study, we are also enemies of God. How can we fix this? We need a hero. And that hero is Jesus.

1. Put the names of the follwing women on the timeline below, where their stories fit.
   - Eve (Genesis 1–5)
   - Tamar (Genesis 38)
   - Rahab (Joshua 2)
   - Ruth (the Book of Ruth)
   - Bathsheba (2 Samuel 11)
   - Mary (Book of Luke)

Eve ──────────────────────────── *Mary*

Creation   Christ's birth

When God put Adam and Eve into Eden, they were living in Eden under a "covenant of works." This meant that as long as they kept God's rules about the Garden, they could stay. They enjoyed a relationship with the Creator Himself along with the

> "In the Old Testament the New is concealed, in the New the Old is revealed."
>
> —Augustine[2]

joys of tending to and living in Paradise, but when they broke the rule and ate from the tree of the knowledge of good and evil (Gen. 2:17), Paradise was lost. Thankfully, before light and dark were created, the Trinity (Father, Son, and Holy Spirit) had made a "covenant of redemption" among themselves. The Trinity had agreed that Eve's mess would not be the last word.

2. How does looking back at the Fall and how God answered Adam and Eve's sin in the Garden make you feel today?

   Righteous loving god → hope.
   Grateful → relief that my saving is not depending on the covent of work but of grace and redemption.

3. Why do you think He did not start over with a fresh creation?

   He seems to love us.
   It did not take him by surprise.
   God does not make mistakes so no need to start over.

Day Two: God's Story

God the Father put into motion a plan that His Son Jesus would pay the price for our sin. Jesus would die in our place, as pictured by the Old Testament sacrifices. Before that necessary death on the cross—when He would crush Satan's head (Gen. 3:15), He would come and live a perfect life among us. Then, the Holy

Spirit would apply Jesus's life and death to us so that sinners can experience the intimate friendship with all three members of the Trinity until we ultimately see Jesus in the new heavens and earth (Rev. 21).

> "The Bible is God's self-revelation. We don't 'discover' God; we can't. He's completely other-than us. He's the Creator and we're the created. Any knowledge we have of him is because he has chosen to reveal himself to us—because he wants us to know him!"
> —Courtney Doctor[3]

1. God unfolded His rescue plan over time in the Old Testament. Trace the Covenant of Grace in the passages below. Refer to the separate Big Picture of the Bible Timeline.

Scripture	Original Recipient	God's Specific Promise
Gen. 3:15		
Gen. 8:20-9:17		
Gen. 15, 17:1-8		
Ex. 19–20	Moses	10 commandment
2 Sam. 7:1-16	David	Kingdom made forever
Jer. 31	Isreal	the new covenant

2. In Genesis 15, God promised Abraham _he will be a father to a multitude of nations_. According to Galatians 3:29, who are Abraham's heirs?
   If you belong to christ you are an heir to christ

3. In Genesis 17:11, God gave Abraham the covenant sign of _circumcision_. According to Romans 2:28-29, what does God circumcise after Jesus's resurrection?

4. In Exodus 19–20, God gave Moses the __10 comenLments__. How did Jesus fulfill the covenant expectations (Matt. 5:17-18)? __He kept the law.__

5. In 2 Samuel 7:12-16, God promised David __a kindom made for ever__.

6. According to Luke 1:30-33, how does Jesus fulfill that promise?

> "Jesus had lived a perfect life. He had never sinned, never uttered a crass word or failed to take a thought captive. He was righteous where Adam had failed. He had even defeated the ancient serpent that had tricked Adam and Eve back in the garden.
>
> "And now the Holy Spirit was taking what Jesus had accomplished, the righteousness that rightfully belonged to Christ, and was applying it to everyone who believed.
>
> "The Spirit was making dead sinners into living saints.
>
> "Jesus people.
>
> "No longer were they slaves to sin. They were free! They had been transferred from the domain of darkness into the Kingdom of the Beloved Son! Their flesh no longer ruled them; Jesus was their new King!"
>
> —Marcos Ortega[4]

Before sin, God walked in the Garden with Adam and Eve (Gen. 3:8). Imagine hanging out with God as you do with your closest friends, maybe even pointing out how the light comes through the trees or laughing over two spotted lion cubs tousling together nearby. Not only did sin usher in death and a broken creation, but it also shattered the intimacy between God and man. When we lose our loved ones to death now, we struggle to adjust to the new reality of not getting to talk to them about a funny story or ask them a question about a lost recipe. Likewise, Adam and Eve's sin created a chasm in their relationship with God. And it was impossible to bridge. To get back to walking alongside His creation, God would have to do something about this chasm.

> ## *Bible Lagniappe*
> ### What Is Covenant Love?
>
> When God made a covenant with His people, He made a solemn promise to always be their God. This meant living with them in a tent while they camped in the desert on the way to the Promised Land, dwelling in a temple in their more established time as a nation, and finally sacrificing Jesus to make our living together full and free forever when we live with God in the new heavens and new earth (Rev. 21). The word *hesed* denotes this kind of covenant love. This is more than a romantic love, it is a loyal, forever love.

But your next question may be, why would God want to bridge it? Why not just dust off His hands of Adam, Eve, and all of us? In other words, why would God want to hang out with ME? Jesus did not die merely to get us out of hell and stamp "Christian" by our name in the Book of Life. He saved us to walk by His side, to enjoy His company, and to delight in His creation. This is the reality we forget between work deadlines and carpool drop-offs. *This* is why He rescued us—not just to keep us out of hell, to suppress our bad behavior, or to leave us to figure life out on our own. He rescued us to hang out with Him, to enjoy Him. We may struggle to believe that as we wallow in the mundane routines, repeated disappointments, and the world's empty promises, but God saves us, so He can live with us, now and eternally. And, from start to finish, God's Word shows how He accomplishes His plan to get rid of the chasm sin created.

7. Referring back to the chart on the Covenant of Grace (p. 30), share how at least one covenant promise comforts you in the messiness of life.

Day Three: Your Story

1. Imagine your story on the timeline. Extend the timeline on page 28 and add your name where it fits.

2. Look up Acts 7:1-54. This is Stephen's sermon, and it summarizes God's rescue plan as presented in the Old Testament.
    a. Who is "the Just One" Stephen mentions?
       Jesus
    b. How would you have responded to Stephen's sermon that day?
       Nothing can stop the promises of god.

> "And you come to the Bible knowing that it's not mostly a book about you and what you're supposed to be doing. It's most of all a story. It's this wonderful love story—about a God who loves his children with a wonderful, never-stopping-never-giving-up-unbreaking-always-and-forever love."
>
> —Sally Lloyd-Jones[5]

Today, if you confess your sins to God and believe Jesus's offer to save you from your messiness, you are part of this story too. And the best part is we know how it ends. Jesus made sure to fulfill all the promises given to God's people in the Covenant of Grace. Those promises included the loyal kind of love that never stops. God will never desert His people, no matter how bad they act. Despite our messy records, we get the benefits of a perfect life, the one Jesus lived in our place. As the "Second Adam" (Rom. 5:12-17), Jesus fulfilled the demands of the Covenant of Works, the obedience the first Adam missed.

The Old and New Testaments are one story interrupted by an intermission that lasted four hundred years. While we get to see this rescue plan neatly labeled on a timeline or read quickly in bedtime Bible stories, the people we read about in the Bible had to wait in real time just like we do today. Abraham spent around twenty-five years in Canaan before Isaac, the son of promise, was born. The Israelites were enslaved for centuries before God sent Moses to their rescue. We forget that to these men and women, God seemed to take a really long time to keep His promises. Like us, they cried over infertility. Like us, they got weary of hoping. They were often mistreated while they waited, but God never stopped working His plan, and He even used the women listed in Matthew 1 in His rescue story. While we are not mothers of the Messiah as they were, He continues to use women like us in His salvation plan for the world. That is where *your* story comes in.

3. What is something you are waiting on God to do in your story today?

4. What gives you hope to be patient?

Bible Lagniappe
Let's Do the Math

How long did Abram wait on God to keep His promise that he'd have children? In Genesis 12, God called Abram to leave his home as well as promised him that he would be a great nation. Abram was childless at this time. By Genesis 16:3, Abram had spent ten years in Canaan. Abram was 86 (Gen. 16:16). Fast forward thirteen years (Gen. 17:1), Abram was 99 and still had no child with his wife, Sarai, who was around 90 years old (Gen. 17:17). But God gave them each new names (Abraham and Sarah), and by the next year (Gen. 21:5), this elderly couple, Abraham (100) and Sarah (90) held their baby, Isaac.

God uses individuals like these five women—and like us—in His grand rescue as He gives us talents, resources, and even trials. He also gives us a purpose: to glorify Him in all we do, big or small.

When my daddy would drop me off at school, he'd yell as I climbed out the car, "Do all for the glory of God!" Although I was embarrassed my friends would overhear this odd goodbye, Daddy's mantra stuck. Years later, whether I was folding laundry or working a boring retail shift, his words came to mind. Anything

I do, I have a purpose that brings joy. And, as God grabs our hearts to glorify Him, we begin the miraculous transformation of enjoying His presence and gifts, trusting Him in all kinds of circumstances, and serving Him faithfully with our hearts and hands. Because Jesus's sacrifice paid off our sins' debt and because His pure life was adjudicated to our account, we will inherit what Jesus earned, an eternal inheritance. We will walk again with God as Adam and Eve did, in the Garden, in the new heavens and new earth (Rev. 21:1-4). Our messiness and our world's messiness will not stop God's plan from happening (Rom. 8:38). And, by the end of God's story for mankind, He will have put us in an even better Eden.

Q. 1: What is the chief end of man?

A: Man's chief end is to glorify God and to enjoy Him forever.[6]

5. How have you seen God use your story to accomplish His promises for those around you?

Memory Verse

For by grace you have been saved through faith. And this is not your own doing; it is the gift of God, not a result of works, so that no one may boast (Eph. 2:8-9).

[1] O. Palmer Robertson, *Christ of the Covenants* (Philipsburg, NJ: P&R Publishing, 1980), 4.

[2] St. Augustine, *Quaestiones in Heptateuchum VII* (Seven Questions Concerning the Heptateuch Dated AD 419-420) 2,73: PL 34, 623; cf. DV 16.

[3] Courtney Doctor, "How the Bible's Story Intersects with Our Story," *enCourage* (blog), September 7, 2020, https://encourage.pcacdm.org/2020/09/07/post-template-213-62/.

[4] Marcos Ortega, "A Kingdom of Jesus People," *Reformed Margins* (blog) March 13, 2018, https://reformedmargins.com/kingdom-jesus-people/.

[5] Sally Lloyd-Jones as quoted by Jonathan Peterson in "The Jesus Storybook Bible: An Interview with Sally Lloyd-Jones," *Bible Gateway* (blog), April 13, 2017, https://www.biblegateway.com/blog/2017/04/the-jesus-storybook-bible-an-interview-with-sally-lloyd-jones/.

[6] *Westminster Shorter Catechism with Scripture Proofs* (Lawrenceville, GA: PCA Committee on Discipleship Ministries, 2010), 3.

Notes

3
The Desperate Daughter-in-Law

I don't know of a children's Bible storybook that includes Tamar's story, and understandably so—it's a little racy for the elementary Sunday school set. Yet, in Matthew 1:3, God introduces His Son's genealogy with this woman who was so desperate, she tricked her father-in-law into fathering her children. It's the kind of story we expect to find on a serial podcast, not in the Bible. But it's there—recorded for all to see—in Genesis 38.

Bible Lagniappe
I Want a Baby!

Infertility is as old as the book of Genesis! For centuries God has heard cries of women wanting to have children. In Bible times this cry was for more than a baby to hold but for their cultural shame to be taken away. A childless woman was seen as a lesser woman, one who must have sinned or not been in God's favor. And, if she did not have a child, especially a son, who would take care of her as she grew older? Being childless was a lonely place to be, and desperate women can do crazy things. See just how desperate two sisters were for children in Genesis 19:32-36.

What's SHE Doing Here?

Day One: Her Story

Read Genesis 38.
1. Why do you think Tamar was desperate, and who was to blame for her situation?

   Shame, social pressure, the call of nature of a woman: to be a mother
   Judah and himself

2. According to Deuteronomy 25:5-6, what was Tamar's recourse for getting help?

   It was her "right" to bear children from her brother in law.

3. How did God provide for Tamar?

   She was not burned
   But wicked men to death

Bible Lagniappe
The Law after the Fact?

Moses (who lived *after* Judah and Tamar) wrote the first five books of the Bible (called the Pentateuch) including the law Judah and his sons broke in Tamar's story. How are Judah and his sons wrong if the law written by Moses in Leviticus came after the fact? Scholars believe this law may have already been in force in the (Abrahamic) covenant community and passed orally from generation to generation. Judah's words in Genesis 38:8 indicate he had an understanding of this law. Thus, the Levitical law codified something God had already revealed to His people.

Can you imagine being in Tamar's shoes? She had married into a "nice Israelite family." Judah was the fifth son of Jacob, and he would become the father of kings (Gen. 49:10), but this man of the covenant had quit keeping the covenant laws in regards to Tamar after losing his two oldest sons (Deut. 25:4-6). He saw Tamar as a bad luck bride, and he conveniently kept her out of sight. However, Tamar used Judah's sinful weaknesses to provide a family for herself. Ironically, her name became a blessing among His people even though her actions were shocking (Ruth 4:11-12).

> "While I am often tempted to look away from the evil and injustice in our world, Jesus never did. He looked. He saw."
> —Vanessa Hawkins[1]

4. Define *grace*.

   to give love to someone who does need but not deserve it.

Read Ruth 4:11-12.

5. What do these verses tell us about God's grace towards Tamar? towards His people?

   He did not leave her even when she sined

6. Describe some times you have experienced God's grace in your life.

   when I did not believe

Day Two: God's Story

As we back up and look at the big picture, we can see that Tamar's story reaches far past her biological clock—this story isn't just about God fixing Tamar's problems. God is weaving together a family line that is off to a rough start but ends in redemption. And that redemption not only includes a family but God's entire creation (Isa. 65:17-25).

> *For behold, I create new heavens and a new earth;*
> *And the former things will not be remembered or come to*
> *mind* (Isa. 65:17).

1. Based on Ruth 4:18-22 and Matthew 1:1-17 fill in the branches of Judah and Tamar's family tree: Tamar & Judah, Perez, Boaz, Obed, Jesse, King David & Bathsheba, Solomon, Joseph & Mary, Jesus.

_____

_____   _____

_____

_____   _____

_____

_____

_____

_____

___Judah___   ___Tamar___

2. Why do you think Jesus is called the "root of Jesse" in Isaiah 11:10?

3. Look up Acts 2:29-30. How did Jesus Christ fulfill the prophecy about Judah and Tamar's descendants given in Genesis 49:8-12?

4. Jesus does not fail us as Judah failed Tamar. How does this give you comfort in your needy places today?

In Tamar's story we see God's signature move of using the unlikely to make His story happen. Over and over, we see Him using the disenfranchised, the unseen, the least powerful as instruments of love and hope. Today, we can feel our lives are too mundane or messed up to be part of His grand salvation. Yet, the Bible shows how He takes our overwhelmingly difficult and unfair situations and weaves them into His good plan to ultimately unite all things into a just and beautiful world.

5. How has God provided for you in spite of your sins, mistakes, or others' unfair treatment of you?

Tamar took a big gamble on sleeping with her father-in-law. After all, she was almost killed as punishment for getting pregnant out of wedlock, but she won big. Did she know she was going to be the mother of the royal line? Probably not. But she knew that God's law was on her side. Even Judah admitted Tamar had been more righteous than he (Gen. 38:26). Judah did not fulfill his obligations as the family leader, and when obedience to God's law became too risky, he chose to protect his family name rather than Tamar. God would not be thwarted by Judah's sin, by Tamar's trick, or by their incestuous liaison. God took a hypocritical man and a desperate woman and made them parents of twin boys, born in unusual circumstances (maybe a hint to how His Son was to be born?) as He developed the royal line towards the Prince of Peace (Isa. 9:6-7).

> "God uses crooked sticks to draw straight lines."
> —Portuguese proverb[2]

Day Three: Your Story

1. Name ways women today may experience unfair treatment.

2. Describe a time when you experienced an unfair situation. How did you feel about God at the time?

Have you ever been in a place as desperate as Tamar's? Today, women do not have to be married or have a son to survive, yet women find themselves in broken homes, unjust communities, and scary places emotionally, physically, and financially. Even in some of our churches, women can feel that the leaders, like Judah, are not being faithful to God's laws, while some members pay the cost.

> "Virtue knows no color line."
> —Ida B. Wells[3]

Tamar found the security she needed in clinging to God's covenant promises. His promises ended up providing for her, even when those in leadership did not. We, like Tamar, must lean into the character of God and His promises. He is our God of justice who cares for widows (Ps. 68:5) and even knows how much hair we may be pulling out on any given day (Matt. 10:30).

3. Look up the following passages and list what you learn about the character of God:

- Deuteronomy 10:18
  A just god + loving god

- Isaiah 30:18
  patient, gracious, merciful, justice, compassion

- James 5:11
  compassion, merciful, blesses the ones who remain steadfast → faithful

- Luke 1:72
  mercy, faithful

- Romans 3:3
  faithful

4. Describe how you see these same character traits in the way God acted in Tamar's story in Genesis 38.

   He remains faithful even when we are unfaithful.

5. Which trait is particularly comforting to you when you are struggling, and why?

   patience
   compassion

We don't know all the thoughts and emotions which caused Judah to renege on marrying his last living son to Tamar, but it's easy to imagine him excusing away his responsibility to Tamar out of a desire to preserve his surviving son. Notice that when Tamar brought his disobedience to the law of God to light, Judah saw the evil of his actions. He repented and submitted to the Lord's ways. Tamar's mess actually helped clean up Judah's. Her pregnancy gave Judah the royal line he could not have guaranteed for himself. Sometimes, we as women act like Judah did. We ignore others' needs because they inconvenience us or threaten our interests.

6. Name examples of women who may be "modern day Tamars."

7. Look up the following passages and write down ways the church, or you, may ignore those women as Judah ignored Tamar.

- Matthew 5:40
  God asks us to . . *Share*

  Excuses to sidestep inconvenient obedience:
  I am lacking things to.

- Matthew 10:40-42
  God asks us to . . *host people, sharing the gosspel*

  Excuses to sidestep inconvenient obedience:
  I'm drained

- Galatians 6:1
  God asks us to . . .

  Excuses to sidestep inconvenient obedience:

- Romans 12:9
  God asks us to . . .

  Excuses to sidestep inconvenient obedience:

- Zechariah 8:16
  God asks us to . . .

  Excuses to sidestep inconvenient obedience:

- 1 Peter 4:8
  God asks us to . . .

Excuses to sidestep inconvenient obedience:

8. According to Psalm 51:17, how can you find strength to forgive those who have hurt you or repent of the harm you've done to others?

> "Fear drive us to do terrible things. And fear that we will lose our own protection, power, and influence has led us and will lead us down a dark path. We must practice humility, serving others, seeking the welfare of others more than ourselves, knowing at every step that this will lead to the suffering of the Church."
> —Marcos Ortega[4]

The fact that our King of grace comes from a family line which includes Tamar's narrative can give hope to us today when our lives or the lives of our loved ones take a messy turn. This genealogy also includes the villain of her story, Judah, who failed Tamar. Christ claims both as "family."

Whether we find ourselves in Tamar's or Judah's sandals, God uses our unusual stories and failures, continually weaving a redemption plot line. Malachi 3:6 says, "For I the LORD do not change; therefore you, O children of Jacob, are not consumed." If that is true, the way God treated Tamar and Judah in Genesis 38 is how He treats us today. We have a King who is forgiving, unchangeable, and who even understands how it feels to be afflicted, overwhelmed, and alone (Heb. 4:15).

> *"For we do not have a high priest who is unable to sympathize with our weaknesses, but one who in every respect has been tempted as we are, yet without sin"* (Heb. 4:15).

9. So, how do you need a King today?

The Valley of Vision[5]

Lord, high and holy, meek and lowly,
Thou has brought me to the valley of vision,
where I live in the depths but see Thee in the heights;
hemmed in by mountains of sin I behold
Thy glory.

Let me learn by paradox
that the way down is the way up,
that to be low is to be high,
that the broken heart is the healed heart,
that the contrite spirit is the rejoicing spirit,
that the repenting soul is the victorious soul,
that to have nothing is to possess all,
that to bear the cross is to wear the crown,
that to give is to receive,
that the valley is the place of vision.

Lord, in the daytime stars can be seen from
deepest wells,
deepest wells,
and the deeper the wells the brighter
Thy stars shine;

Let me find Thy light in my darkness,
Thy life in my death,
Thy joy in my sorrow,
Thy grace in my sin,
Thy riches in my poverty
Thy glory in my valley.

Memory Verse

**Some trust in chariots and some in horses,
but we trust in the name of the Lord our God (Ps. 20:7).**

---

[1] Vanessa Hawkins, "On Oneness, Lament, and Seeing with Compassion," *enCourage* (blog), June 4, 2020, https://encourage.pcacdm.org/2020/06/04/post-template-213-36/.

[2] George Monteiro, "The Literary Uses of a Proverb." *Folklore*, Vol. 87, No. 2 (Abingdon, UK: Taylor & Francis, Ltd. 1976), 216-18.

[3] Ida B. Wells, *The Red Record,* first published in 1895 (New York: Open Road Integrated Media, Inc., 2015), 7.

[4] Marcos Ortega, "Year 501 and Beyond," *Reformed Margins* (blog), October 31, 2018, https://reformedmargins.com/year-501-and-beyond/.

[5] "The Valley of Vision" in *The Valley of Vision*, edited by Arthur Bennett (Edinburgh: Banner of Truth Trust, 1975), xv.

The Desperate Daughter-in-Law

Notes

4
The Career Prostitute

I don't know a lot of prostitutes personally, but God certainly does. Throughout the Bible we meet women who live by selling sex. And, throughout Jesus's time on earth He also knew women whom others would avoid, ignore, or condemn. From the woman avoiding the normal well time in John 4, to the woman with a history of sexual sins in Luke 7:47, women found new lives with Jesus and still can today. When God gives a new heart to a woman, He also gives her a new identity. She is now a daughter of the King, sister of our Big Brother Jesus, reflecting that kind of salvation. Matthew's genealogy includes Rahab, a "lady of the night" who became an Israelite "Woman of the Year."

As we open this passage in Joshua 2, God's people were in the early stages of taking the Promised Land and were facing Jericho's impenetrable walls. Joshua's spies sneaked in and found help in, of all places, the city's red light district. After all, a brothel was a great place to hear the latest rumors and provided the spies intelligence they needed to attack Jericho.

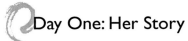Day One: Her Story

Read Joshua 2.
1. Why did Rahab risk her life hiding the spies and helping the enemy?

2. How must women today make similar choices between choosing a life for God or a life against God?

3. What does this choice look like in your life today?

I wonder how hard Rahab's heart was beating when the Jericho CIA banged on her door. What possessed Rahab to risk everything for these two strangers? Sure, her "everything" was a life of prostitution, but this choice meant she was risking it all with a God she had never seen and for a people she didn't know. Her words in Joshua 2:8-13 clue us in.

> "No one is so good that she doesn't need the gospel, and no one is so lost that the gospel can't find her."
> —Melissa B. Kruger[1]

> Before the men lay down, she came up to them on the roof and said to the men, "I know that the LORD has given you the land, and that the fear of you has fallen upon us, and that all the inhabitants of the land melt away before you. For we have heard how the LORD dried up the water of the Red Sea before you when you came out of Egypt, and what you did to the two kings of the Amorites who were beyond the Jordan, to Sihon and Og, whom you devoted to destruction. And as soon as we heard it, our hearts melted, and there was no spirit left in any man because of you, for the LORD your God, he is God in the heavens above and on the earth beneath. Now then, please swear to me by the LORD that, as I have dealt kindly with you, you also

will deal kindly with my father's house, and give me a sure sign that you will save alive my father and mother, my brothers and sisters, and all who belong to them, and deliver our lives from death."

Rumors had been flying around Jericho. She had heard about this God, a God who parted seas, overthrew governments, and stuck to this people named Israel. The strong walls of Jericho could not provide what she needed—safety and salvation. So, she bet her life on Someone who could deliver her from death and give her a new life. She chose to follow the God of Israel.

4. What are "strong cities" you are trusting in to give you security?

5. What is the risk versus the reward for you choosing God over that "strong city"?

6. What did Rahab believe specifically about God (Josh. 2:8-13)?

7. Write some things you believe about God today.

"Like a woman in labor, Jesus fixed his eyes on the prize at the end, and he endured. With every crack of the whip, Jesus focused on your face. With every staggering step, he set his heart on you and put one foot in front of the other. When he fell under the weight of his cross, he stood up, because he needed to save you. When the final, most devastating blow came, when he experienced hell on the cross, he screamed in agony. But he didn't leave. He stayed. For you, child of God, were the joy set before him."

—Abby Hutto[2]

 Day Two: God's Story

Read Joshua 6.

1. How does God's judgment on Jericho make you feel?

2. Who else besides Rahab was saved?

3. How does your faith in God and actions impact others?

Imagine the tension as Jericho watched the Israelites march around the city, day after day. Finally, the trumpets blew, the strong walls tumbled down, and the Israelites destroyed every living thing. Yet, in the middle of the carnage, the spies kept their promise, grabbed Rahab and her family, and took them to a safe distance from the destruction. Against the harsh judgment day for Jericho, we see God's salvation of a harlot's family shine.

4. How do you feel about God's judgment on Jericho in Joshua 6?

5. According to Genesis 15:16, why were the inhabitants of Jericho doomed?

6. What does the annihilation of Jericho teach you about God's wrath and judgment?

7. What does the escape of Rahab's family teach you about God's grace?

> "By their simple and repeated use of the term 'brothers' (or 'brothers and sisters'), the writers of the Epistles underscore that the people in the pews around us are, in fact, our family. Like the members of our biological family, we haven't chosen them for ourselves, but they have been chosen for us, and we are therefore inseparably bound to them. Because we are allied with Christ, we are allied with his family."
> —Megan Hill[3]

Seeing God's judgment on Jericho is tough to put into perspective when this kind of destruction affected the innocent along with the guilty. Is this the same God who gives us the psalms and stories of love and gentle care? As we watch the accumulation of sin cost the complete annihilation of Jericho, we get clued into how awful and costly sin itself is. Our culture is far from calling out sin for what it is. Even in our personal lives, we dismiss our sins as shortcomings or mistakes. In order to not feel the weight of our wrongs, we lighten sin's load. However, whether we as a culture or as individuals do this, we are still guilty. Still accountable. "For in the hand of the LORD there is a cup with foaming wine, well mixed, and he pours out from it, and all the wicked of the earth shall drain it down to the dregs" (Ps. 75:8). But that is where this rescue of Rahab and her family points to the gospel hope of rescue. Yes, our sins cost a lot, but Jesus took that frothy, stinky cup and drank it down to its dregs on the cross. And then . . . He not only rescues us like He did Rahab, but He says, "You are

---

Bible Lagniappe
God Loves a Family Connection

God loves to work His salvation out in families. Rahab's family was included in the Jericho rescue because they were with Rahab when the spies came back. When the Philippian jailer (Acts 16:30-31) asked Paul and Silas how to be saved, they said, "Believe in the Lord Jesus, and you will be saved, you and your household." Today, many churches baptize babies as a sign that they are included in the family of faith, looking forward to the time they will profess Christ as their Savior. No matter what your family of origin looks like, God makes us all (singles, widows, divorcées, orphans, moms, or wives) family. His family. So then you are no longer strangers and aliens, but you are fellow citizens with the saints and members of the household of God (Eph. 2:19).

free," and He makes us part of His family. Can you imagine the family who accepted not only an enemy, a Jericho citizen, but also welcomed her in marriage? That is exactly what God does to the Rahabs of the world, to us with all our sins. He gives us a new family name, a new life, and a new identity (Eph. 2:19).

Day Three: Your Story

1. Read James 2:25. *Why* did Rahab do what she did?

2. Read Hebrews 11:31. *How* did she do what she did?

My dad taught me to "proof my yeast" before using it in a recipe. That means I add the yeast packet to warm water and see if bubbles come up. If it doesn't, my yeast won't work when I bake. In Rahab's story her faith "got proofed" by her actions. Hiding the spies, putting her life in the spies' hands, convincing her family to join her were "bubbles" proving her faith in God was real. Compare her escape from Jericho's judgment to Lot's wife's in the judgment of Sodom (Gen. 19:12-26). Both women showed their faith by their actions. One escaped judgment and one did not. This is pretty scary, and I don't want to end up a pillar of salt or facing the wrong side of God's judgment. Although Rahab had earned judgment like her fellow citizens, something happened that saved her. She just had to leave her old life for a new one. That kind of faith is a gift.

> Definition of grace:
> "Unmerited divine assistance given to humans for their regeneration or sanctification"[4]

3. What is it you need to leave behind to follow God?

4. What are signs of "proofing" your faith which you see in your life today?

5. What gift of faith do you want to ask God for today?

Bible Lagniappe
From Old Testament Hooker to New Testament Role Model

Rahab shows up later in the New Testament when two different writers bring her up as an example of faith. James says that Rahab proved her faith was real by hiding the spies. The writer of Hebrews put Rahab in his "Faith Hall of Fame" when he said she avoided judgment and death with Jericho when she chose God's side by hiding the spies (Heb. 11:31).

Our stories are not always easy to tell. We find ourselves saddled with consequences of our sinful choices and wonder if we will ever be worthy of belonging to a loving God. We wonder if we can become a part of the church community which talks about a holy God wanting a holy people. Rahab reminds us that our belonging to His people comes from the faith that God gives, not a perfect past we bring. Many women feel disqualified as "real" Christians because they have a checkered past. Jesus was pretty comfortable forgiving women with a past as seen in Luke 7:47: "Therefore I tell you, her sins, which are many, are forgiven—for she loved much. But he who is forgiven little, loves little." Jesus did not dismiss her sins or act like she was just misguided or didn't know better. He admitted she had a past, but He forgave her sins. And that past was erased by grace.

> **One Drop of Blood**
> Translation of one of the hymns sung by Cherokee
> American Indians on the Trail of Tears[5]
>
> What can we do, Jesus, our King? He's already paid for us.
> Our friends, we all must work.
> Our King, Your place over which You are King.
> Our King, Your place over which You are King.

Rahab's life was messy. Yours may be too. But lifestyles of past sexual sin do not disqualify us from serving our God. Maybe you are scared to trust God with your sexual scars and join a body of believers. Ask Him to make your heart brave like Rahab's. When you look in the mirror, you may see a sinner full of sexual scars, but by faith, can you better see the woman forgiven, a precious and pure sister of her Savior Jesus?

Perhaps you do not bear the brunt of past sexual sins, but how are you welcoming those with these wounds into your present life? Is your church open-armed to those who struggle with same-sex attraction? Are you coming alongside the single mom taking care of children with multiple fathers? Do your corporate prayer times include prayers for the mothers who aborted their children? Or do you keep the messy people like Rahab at arm's length? Do you invite them to eat at your table as Jesus did (Matt. 9:11)? Rahab's past did not stop her from joining the people of God, and it did not stop God's people from accepting her. Was it easy? I bet it was very hard. But God Himself saved her to be a "mother of the Messiah" instead of "Rahab the harlot," clearing the way for us messy women to be called "daughters of God."

> Arise, my soul, arise! Shake off thy guilty fears;
> The bleeding Sacrifice in my behalf appears.
> Before the throne my Surety stands;
> My name is written on his hands.
> —Charles Wesley[6]

6. Read Psalm 25:8-11. Fill in the blanks.

"Good and upright is the Lord; Therefore He instructs _____ in the way. He leads the _____ in what is right, and teaches the _____ his way. All the paths of the Lord are steadfast _____ and _____, for those who keep his covenant and his testimonies. For your name's sake, O Lord, _____ my _____, for it is _____."

7. How is your church or Bible study making church life accessible to those women who struggle with sexual sins or consequences of sexual sins?

8. What are specific improvements you could make to make your spaces more welcoming?

9. How do the "Rahabs" help "God's kingdom come" in your current setting?

> "But when I came to Christ, I experienced what nineteenth-century Scottish theologian Thomas Chalmers called 'the expulsive power of a new affection.' At the time of my conversion, my lesbian identity and feelings did not vanish. As my union with Christ grew, the sanctification that it birthed put a wedge between my old self and my new one. In time, this contradiction exploded, and I was able to claim identity in Christ alone."
>
> —Rosaria Butterfield[7]

This lesson challenges us to change in some pretty deep places. Whether we are the one who needs gospel love or we are God's tools to give it, how is that change possible? The same way all believe and act upon that gospel truth—*through God's power*. Historically, the Church has failed to meet people well in their sexual struggles, and while we want our communities of faith to reflect God's grace, we are Christians who do not always act like Christ. How are we to improve? I'm relieved to say, Someone outside of us promises to help. God Himself gives us power to believe, discernment to act, and grace to walk in ways that honor Him (Col. 1:10-12).

> But we never can prove
> The delights of His love
> Until all on the altar we lay;
> For the favor He shows,
> For the joy He bestows,
> Are for them who will trust and obey.
>
> —John H. Sammis[8]

> ## *Bible Lagniappe*
> ### Jesus, a Friend of Sinners
>
> Jesus was not scared to associate with prostitutes or women with a past of sexual sins. In John 4, He captured a rest at a well with a woman who had been married several times and was living with a man. In Luke 7:37, Jesus praised the physical worship of the prostitute washing His feet (after the rude welcoming of His host, Simon, a religious leader). And when an adulterous woman was brought to Jesus, He was quick to forgive her sins while the men in charge were quick to stone her (John 8:1-11). When Jesus was asked in Matthew 9:11-13 (NIV), why He hung out with sinners, He replied, "For I have not come to call the righteous, but sinners."

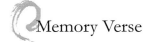
Memory Verse

Jesus said to him, "I am the way, and the truth, and the life. No one comes to the Father except through me" (John 14:6).

---

[1] Melissa B. Kruger, *In All Things: A Nine Week Devotional Bible Study on Unshakeable Joy* (New York, NY: Multnomah, 2018), 21.

[2] Abby Hutto, "The Prayers of Our Savior," *God for Us* (blog), April 9, 2020, https://www.godforusministries.com/o-wide-embracing-wondrous-love/2020/4/9/the-prayers-of-our-savior.

[3] Megan Hill, *A Place to Belong: Learning to Love the Local Church* (Wheaton, IL: Crossway, 2020), 106.

[4] https://www.merriam-webster.com/dictionary/grace.

[5] According to Charlotte Heth in "Cherokee Hymn Singing in Oklahoma," *1992 Festival of American Folklife Program* (Washington, D.C.: Smithsonian Institution, 1992), 95-97.

⁶ Charles Wesley, "Arise My Soul Arise," *Trinity Hymnal* (Suwanee, GA: Great Commission Publications, 2018), 305.

⁷ Rosaria Butterfield as quoted in "An Unlikely Convert: An Interview with Rosaria Butterfield," *Tabletalk Magazine*, April 1, 2015, https://www.ligonier.org/learn/articles/unlikely-convert/.

⁸ John H. Sammis, "Trust and Obey," *Trinity Hymnal* (Suwanee, GA: Great Commission Publications, 2018), 672.

Notes

5
The Ultimate Outsider

Women find themselves in scary places. Financial dependence, emotional emptiness, and wounds of heartbreaking losses can hamstring a woman's hopes for safety and security. God gives us the book of Ruth, so we can see how He provides and loves broken and even bitter women, using them to provide and love His people in the greater story.

> "Loneliness. That's the word that comes to mind when I (Michelle) think back to eating lunch in my school's cafeteria as a kid. I was that girl; the girl who no one wanted to sit with; the girl who people made fun of; the girl who, perhaps, people feared.
>
> While everyone else was eating PB&J sandwiches and apple slices, I brought my delicious leftover Indian food. Whether it was chicken curry or aloo gobi and rotis, I would pull it out with a sense of pride, eager to eat my mom's homemade dishes. But what smelled and tasted like heaven to me was a disgust to my peers. I remember the boys calling it "throw up" and the girls whispering to each other, while pointing and laughing.
>
> My ethnic otherness, from the food I ate to the clothes my family wore and the color of my skin, made me an outsider. I didn't have many friends at school. But, oh, how I longed for people to step outside of their culture and enter into my own. I longed for people to cross their culture to me, to extend a hand of friendship and to love me for who I was—an East Indian gal with dark hair and brown skin."
>
> —Michelle Reyes[1]

Day One: Her Story

Read the book of Ruth to get the whole story, although we will focus only on Ruth 1 in this lesson.

We do not know who wrote the book of Ruth, but it is set during the period of Israelite history when judges, not kings, ruled. Judges 21:25 sums up that time well, "in those days there was no king in Israel. Everyone did what was right in his own eyes." Sound familiar?

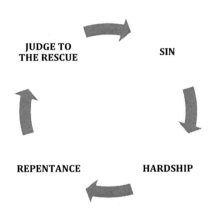

Whenever that happened and because part of being in relationship with God is His correction, God sent hardship on His people so they would return to Him. The people would cry out for help and repent, and God would send a judge to rescue them. Perhaps the famine in Naomi's day was a time of God's disciplining His people so they would return to Him.

1. What happened to Naomi's family, and how is Naomi related to Ruth?

2. According to Ruth 1:9, what does Naomi want these two women to find and where would they typically find it?

3. By choosing to go with Naomi, with whom else does Ruth choose to live?

When our children need bread, we women will do anything to get it. I wonder what Naomi thought as Elimelech, their sons, and she pulled out of Bethlehem, leaving their hometown for the hope of bread in Moab. Ironically, Bethlehem means "house of bread," and the book opens with this small family trading the normal place of God's blessings for a foreign country, Moab. Moab did what it could and lived up to its advertisements of literal bread, but it proved to be a poor refuge for God's people. By verse 5 and over a decade later, we see Naomi's husband and two married sons were dead.

This was a big problem for Naomi and her daughters-in-law. After all, a widow with no men had little financial stability or physical protection. Bitter and empty, Naomi packed her bags to return home. Her loyal and caring daughters-in-law, Orpah and Ruth, begged to go with her. Naomi knew that her life would be hard back home as an Israelite widow, but life for her daughters-in-law, as foreign widows—even harder. They would be outsiders. A son of a Moabite could not even worship like other men in Israel. "Go back," Naomi said, "and find rest in the home of a Moabite husband."

4. From Naomi's perspective (1:9), "rest" would come through a husband's or family's protection and support. How do women today find "rest"?

5. Fill in the blanks of Ruth 1:21.

"I went away _____, and the Lord has brought me back _____. Why call me Naomi, when the Lord has testified _____ me and the Almighty has brought _____ upon me?"

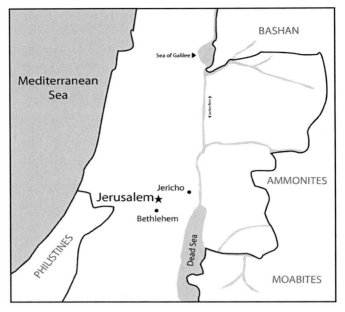

6. If Naomi knew that God had been part of hers and Ruth's difficult story, why were they going toward God and His people?

> *He executes justice for the orphan and the widow, and shows His love for the alien by giving him food and clothing* (Deut. 10:18).

 Day Two: God's Story

Go back and read Ruth 1:16-17.

1. What did Ruth commit to doing?

2. Compare Ruth's words to God's words to Abraham in Genesis 12:1-3 and Jesus's departing words to His followers in Matthew 28:18-20.

Ruth 1:16-17	Genesis 12:1-3	Matthew 28:18-20

3. List similar themes you see in the passages above:

As Ruth vowed to stick to Naomi and her God, the words reflect what God Himself swore to Abraham centuries before. Ruth's words and God's words sound familiar because they are both talking about a relationship. She vowed loyalty to Naomi even if it would cost her. God vowed loyalty to us knowing that relationship would cost Him His only Son, Jesus.

> "There are better things ahead than any we leave behind."
> —C.S. Lewis[2]

But why did Ruth and Naomi go toward this God when Naomi admitted He had afflicted her? Why go toward a God who would allow this kind of heartache? The best answer I can give you is to quote Peter's words in John 6:68, "Lord, to whom shall we go? You have the words of eternal life." As you look over all of the stories woven together into God's Big Story of salvation, you see that hardship is par for the course. Even Jesus suffered when He lived among us. But as death and its impact is part of our stories, we also know The Bigger Story will end beautifully, making all the tears worth it. God's promises will come true. And now that Naomi's and Ruth's arms were truly empty, they had more incentive to reach towards God's promises to fill them.

> "If God sends us on strong paths, we are provided strong shoes."
> —Corrie ten Boom[3]

Have you ever seen a nest of baby birds? They squawk and do nothing but open their beaks, waiting for a worm to be delivered by Mama Bird. Psalm 81:10 says, "I am the LORD your God, who brought you up out of the land of Egypt. Open your mouth wide, and I will fill it." This is what Ruth and Naomi did. They moved towards a God with a track record of saving and filling mouths of undeserving people. And, like Peter, we cannot think of a better plan.

4. Name your empty places.

5. Write down aspects of God's character found in the following passages:
   - Deuteronomy 4:31

   - Joel 2:13

   - Psalm 94:14

- Isaiah 41:10-13

- Hebrews 10:23

6. Look up Job 13:15. Name the scary things God may allow into your life for your good.

7. Circle the attributes of God listed in the verses above (#5) that help you trust Him even if it looks like He will allow the things you just listed to happen in your life.

Day Three: Your Story

Ruth made a big decision at the crossroads that day. Would she follow a bitter mother-in-law to a foreign land where life would be against her *or* stay in Moab with her hometown advantage for an easier life? What made her take the harder path? Why would any woman do what Ruth did?

Naomi put her finger on the crux of the decision when she said, "See, your sister-in-law has gone back to her people and to her gods; return after your sister-in-law" (Ruth 1:15). Did Ruth really want to leave behind her gods, her hometown, her comfort zone to follow Naomi and the God of Israel? Would God be enough for Ruth as she left all she had known to become an outsider in Israel?

1. Look up Matthew 13:45-46. How do you see Ruth living out this parable?

The "rest" of work credentials, comfortable homes, and beautiful families will last as long as Moab's did for Naomi and Ruth. It can only take us so far and fill our desires so much, leaving us vulnerable to bitterness, emptiness, and frustration later. Nothing and no one besides God can give us what we truly need to feel our feet on solid ground that does not shift (Matt. 7:24-27). Although Bethlehem did not seem to offer a lot to Ruth, empty with God is better than full without Him. Like the merchant who sold all to buy the great pearl (Matt. 13:45-46), Ruth's decision made all the sense in the world to her.

> "What does it look like to surrender to Christ, to cast our cares on the Lord (Ps. 55:22)? For me, it means running to Jesus before I run to news outlets and social media. It means loosening my grip on what I think needs to be done and how I think it should happen, walking instead in the counter-cultural ways of His Spirit through prayer and time in His word. It means believing in the power of His Church over the influence of government policies and social activism. And it means shutting off my computer and getting the sleep that I need—humbly acknowledging and trusting that though I am finite, my Father is not."
>
> —Grace Liu[4]

2. Where is your rest coming from today?

3. What are the tell-tale signs that it is coming from places other than God?

If I wonder where my "rest" is, I only have to wait until I see my emotions emerge when that thing is threatened. My child's five cavities wreck a purchase for a new outfit. I struggle to congratulate my co-worker's job promotion because I get scared I am not as valued in the office. My crankiness after paying bills belies the fact that I feel more peace on payday than at the end of the month. The good things God gives us—money, jobs, families—were never built to give us life, yet we cling to them as if our lives depend on them.

> *Come to me, all who labor and are heavy laden, and I will give you rest. Take my yoke upon you, and learn from me, for I am gentle and lowly in heart, and you will find rest for your souls. For my yoke is easy, and my burden is light*
> (Matt. 11:28-30).

4. Based on how you respond to certain good things, what do you tend to cling to for "rest?"

5. If you struggle with choosing God over other good things, name specific ways you can respond like Ruth and Naomi instead of like Orpah.

> ## *Bible Lagniappe*
> ### International Intrigue
>
> Moab was a neighboring country of Israel, God's promised land for His people, but Israel and Moab go way back. Remember Lot's daughters' desperation in Genesis 19:37? Those babies turned into countries that competed with Israel. Numbers 22:2-6 provides a little more color commentary on the relationship between Moab and Israel.

Memory Verse

Because he holds fast to me in love, I will deliver him; I will protect him, because he knows my name (Ps. 91:14).

---

[1] Michelle Reyes, "A Theology of Cross-Cultural Relationships," *The Art of Taleh* (blog), January 3, 2019, http://www.theartoftaleh.com/a-theology-of-cross-cultural-friendships/.

[2] C.S. Lewis, letter to Mary Willis Shelburne on June 17, 1963. *The Collected Letters of C.S. Lewis*, Volume 3: Narnia, Cambridge, and Joy, 1950-1963 (London: HarperCollins, 2004), 1430.

[3] Corrie ten Boom. Used with permission by the Corrie ten Boom House Foundation, Haarlem, Holland.

[4] Grace Liu, "Justice, Jesus, and Rest for the Weary," *Asian American Christian Collaborative* (blog), March 23, 2021, https://www.asianamericanchristiancollaborative.com/article/justice-jesus-and-rest-for-the-weary.

Notes

6
From Outsider to Ultimate Insider

Ruth is the "Cinderella Story" of the Old Testament. It seems to be a rags-to-riches narrative and many of us love it for the happy ending. Boaz seemed to be every bit the hero as Elizabeth's Mr. Darcy, Beauty's Beast, and Snow White's Prince Charming (though in this story, a covenant is sealed, not with a kiss, but with a sandal). Ruth's story is a good one and a *true* one, but we'll see that it was much more than just a girl getting her prince.

> "Love is inconvenient. It actually has the audacity to ask us to drop what we're doing in order to attend to the needs of another. It presses up against our desires for autonomy, comfort, ease, safety, and control. It punctures our bubble of self-importance and self-protection. It lifts our heads to look up and outward at our neighbor, instead of down and inward at ourselves. It prods us toward a 'you before me' ethos and away from our fleshly default of 'me before you.' It beckons us to see and live through another's eyes. So Jesus, knowing our hearts, turned our self-interest on its head when he said, 'So whatever you wish that others would do to you, do also to them . . .'" (Matt 7:12).
>
> —Mike Emlet[1]

Day One: Her Story

Read Ruth 2-4.

1. Write what you observe about each person as you read the text.
   - Ruth

   - Naomi

   - Boaz

   - The "closer relative" at the gate

   - The LORD

Bible Lagniappe
What Is a Kinsman-Redeemer?

A kinsman-redeemer was someone in the Old Testament who took responsibility for a family member who needed help or protection. This could have been a widow or poor relative who had to sell family land to survive. This law allowed for generational property to be kept within the family and provided protection for the social or economic injustices that could occur in Israel.

2. What impressed Boaz about Ruth?

3. According to Boaz, who was taking care of Ruth as she lived in a foreign place?

4. Name the specific ways Boaz took care of Ruth in . . .
   • Chapter 2:

   • Chapter 3:

   • Chapter 4:

5. After Ruth and Boaz married and had a son, the women rejoiced with Naomi, saying (4:14-15): "Blessed be the _____, who has not _____ you this day without a redeemer; and may his name be renowned in _____! He shall be to you a _____ of life and a _____ of your old age; for your daughter-in-law, who loves you, who is _____ to you than _____, has given birth to him."

6. Consider last week's lesson when you listed places you go to for "rest" instead of to God. How would you sing along with the Bethlehem ladies? "The LORD who loves you is better than _____."

As you finish reading Ruth, you can almost picture a Broadway show, with Naomi's friends singing the closing number. All is well—the widow has become a wife! Naomi's empty arms hold

> ### *Bible Lagniappe*
> ### God's Hospitality
>
> God has always been hospitable, especially to outsiders. He specifically addressed how His people as a nation should treat immigrants living among them (Lev. 19:34; Deut. 10:19; Ex. 22:21). The big basis for their kind treatment was the fact that God's people themselves had lived for four hundred years in a land not their own. Since they knew how hard it was to be aliens, they should show mercy and justice to the aliens living among them. Later, Paul used the alien or immigrant metaphor when comparing how God has taken us as outsiders and made us ultimate insiders as members of His family (Eph. 2:12, 19).

a baby boy! The story that began in bitterness ends in joy with a giant backdrop of lights spelling out REST as the curtain closes.

It's ironic. As an audience, we see along the way what may have been hard for Naomi and Ruth to see in the moment—that God was always there, behind the scenes, moving and acting. The writer of this book emphasized the obviousness of God's sovereignty by not using His name as the action unfolded. God is a big God and may use all sorts of crazy things to provide for His children. In Moses's day, He sprinkled manna (Ex. 16:4) and He sent ravens with meat and bread to Elijah (1 Kings 17:2-16). But in Ruth and Naomi's story, we see God providing for them using very ordinary means. We do not see Ruth waiting expectantly for UberEats or Naomi checking her Lotto ticket. Instead, we see Ruth getting dressed and going to a barley field, day after day. We see Boaz noticing the new woman in his field and making sure she is protected. Even the bitter Naomi perked up when she heard that Ruth had found help in the field of a close relative. God used the kindness of Boaz, not manna or ravens, to feed two widows. He worked through the everyday laws He had established for taking care of the poor (Lev. 19:9), and He worked through the obedience of Ruth and Boaz who kept more than the letter of the law but also kept the spirit of covenant love.

Not very exciting, but very effective.

7. What are ways God's laws protect and provide for you?

8. Describe ways people show you the covenant love of God through ordinary means.

> "When you have a party—Christmas party, birthday party, or some other significant event—invite those who *can't repay you*. Invite the marginalized. And you will be repaid 'at the resurrection of the just.' Jesus fills up ordinary events with eternal significance."
> —Tony Merida[2]

 Day Two: God's Story

Read Ruth 4.

You may think some of the details of Ruth and Boaz's dating are, well, weird. Since when does a guy give a girl a shawl full of barley for an engagement ring? (Not to mention tell her to give it to her mother-in-law—hello!) What about Naomi telling Ruth to dress up and sneak in during the night to lie down at Boaz's

> ## Bible Lagniappe
> ### Like Mother, Like Daughter-in-Law
>
> Boaz was no stranger to, well, *strangers* in Israel. If you visit his family portrait gallery, you will find Boaz's mother, Rahab, the prostitute of our last lesson. No wonder he took care to protect the foreigner in his field. And, because his own mother had been an outsider-made-insider, Boaz considered Ruth a beautiful match due to her covenantal faithfulness to Naomi and her new people.

feet? And, finally, why is Ruth choosing an old man instead of chasing after the younger ones (even Boaz comments on this in 3:10)?

Some of those customs may seem odd to us, but what is so exciting is that this one story reflects the Big Story of the Bible. Boaz represents a type of Christ. In Boaz's role as kinsman-redeemer, we get a peek at what a spiritually romantic rescue looks like. He went to court to buy Ruth's property and take her as his

> "Living in this in-between place lends itself to a peculiar kind of loneliness. I feel the absence of not having a close friend who can commiserate with this part of my life. What if there had been a friend with a similar background like mine while growing up, and we could have shared our common experiences, puzzlements, and frustrations? What if I had such a friend now? It has taken me years to untangle and unpack internal dialogues and assimilation strategies I developed, and years of reckoning and soul-searching to reach a place of peace and rest regarding my identity. Living without friendship in my life has made me a loyal friend, and for those willing to befriend someone who doesn't look like them, I have found true friendship. Some of my closest friends happen to have blond hair—and we happily accept each other as we are."
>
> —Prasanta Verma[3]

wife, thus rescuing Ruth and Naomi. He gave up his right to keep this property under his name and accepted that his firstborn boy would be shared by Ruth's first husband's name. He welcomed a widow who was not only a foreigner, but also one who came with the baggage of another man's mother.

Didn't Jesus do the same for us?

1. Look up the following passages. How do you see Boaz as a shadow of what Jesus does for His Bride?
    - Romans 5:10

    - Ephesians 5:25-27

    - Hebrews 7:22

    - 1 John 2:1

Changed Mah Name[4]

I tol' Jesus it would be all right
If He changed my name

Jesus tol' me I would have to live humble
If He changed mah name

Jesus tol' me that the world would be 'gainst me
If He changed mah name

But I tol' Jesus it would be all right
If He changed mah name

Like Ruth, we are outsiders, even enemies, to God, but Jesus sacrificed His rights in order to make us His family. As Boaz swapped a sandal to seal the marriage with Ruth, Jesus takes His blood to the throne room of God and swaps His life for ours. Jesus gives us a shawl-full of His Spirit as a down payment that this relationship is real and secure as we wait on Him to come back and marry His people in front of all the nations.

> *And he came and preached peace to you who were far off and peace to those who were near. For through him we both have access in one Spirit to the Father. So then you are no longer strangers and aliens, but you are fellow citizens with the saints and members of the household of God* (Eph. 2:17-19).

But do not quit reading Ruth too soon, as today's readers are tempted to skip genealogies. The final verses are a huge hint of why God tells Ruth's story. Ruth was part of something bigger than giving us a feel-good story about an outsider fitting into God's community. As much as God cared deeply for the individuals of this story, He was also taking care of His people *through* this story. The baby Obed meant more than a reversal to Naomi's fortune. Sure, Obed became a "restorer of life" to Naomi, but Ruth's descendant, Jesus, would be the world's Restorer of life. Ruth became the ultimate insider, holding, in a sense, The Baby who holds us all.

> "True worship is the result of one's overflowing gratitude for no longer being on the outside. The woman's action is a microcosm of Christian worship. The Christian life is a grateful response to the God who has brought us 'outsiders' into his arms and made us part of his family."
> —Trevin Wax[5]

Day Three: Your Story

Just as Ruth asked Boaz to "take me under your wing" (Ruth 3:9), we ask God to do the same (Ps. 91:4). Jesus is our Boaz and Bridegroom (Eph. 5:25-27).

1. Look up the following psalms that not only were written by Ruth's great-grandson, David, but also include this family motto of coming under God's wings for refuge. Note what kind of trouble David was in and his verses about sheltering under God's wings.

    - Psalm 17
      David's trouble:

      Verse of shelter:

    - Psalm 36
      David's trouble:

      Verse of shelter:

    - Psalm 57
      David's trouble:

      Verse of shelter:

    - Psalm 63
      David's trouble:

      Verse of shelter:

> "He always knows best what we need most ... even when it's what we like least."
> —Lori Sealy[6]

2. Although you may not be on the run from a King Saul or escaping a coup instigated by your son Absalom, name difficulties you are facing today.

3. Name some ways you see that God keeps you under His wings.

4. From the "wings" verses above, pick one that comforts you, write it out below, and meditate on it this week.

5. What do you risk when you go towards Jesus for your *rest* and *security*?

> "O Lord our God, under the shadow of Thy wings let us hope. Thou wilt support us, both when little, and even to gray hairs. When our strength is of Thee, it is strength; but, when our own, it is feebleness. We return unto Thee, O Lord, that from their weariness our souls may rise towards Thee, leaning on the things which Thou hast created, and passing on to Thyself, who hast wonderfully made them; for with Thee is refreshment and true strength. Amen."
>
> —Augustine[7]

When Ruth came home to Naomi with the load of barley, Naomi was confident Boaz would take care of business by the end of the day (3:18). Likewise, we can trust God to take care of us. And, if Naomi were here, she would tell us to "sit still" while we wait on God's timing as we walk through our hard places. We can be confident within even if we feel shaky, because we know God has that dual combo of strength *and* merciful lovingkindness (Ps. 62:11-12a).

We can still limp into worship and whisper songs of what is true about Him and His final victory. As we read His Word, we can underline the passages that fill our hearts with hope (and maybe even see them years later when we need them again!). On a lonely, hard day, we can murmur a prayer that still falls immediately into the ears of our strong Savior, and He will send His angels to help (Ps. 34:7). When faced with a guilty conscience and sin's power, we can cry out, "Take me under your wing!" and Jesus, in ultimate Hero style, wields a mighty sword to save His own. He gives us the Holy Spirit (Eph. 1:14) as an engagement ring of sorts, like that shawl full of barley Ruth carried home, to remind us of our future wedding feast in Heaven (Rev. 19:7-10).

> "With him, I am secure and loved. And while lingering pain can remain from the rejection of other people, his love removes the sting and the shame. I can rest in him and rejoice in knowing that he will always delight in me."
>
> —Darby Strickland[8]

6. Look up Isaiah 62:2b-5. Name ways Jesus has taken you from "desolate" to "My delight is in her."

> "How can we invite those our Shepherd so desperately wants to exalt? We look for those who are marginalized, silenced, abused, and powerless. We have eyes for the outsider who doesn't have our social capital and we invite them in. Maybe it's the new immigrant family who moved in down the street who is navigating a new city. Maybe it's the special needs child and their weary family who goes to your child's school. Perhaps you invite them not to a meal, but to a conversation and then a friendship. Maybe you find yourself sharing resources with them, buying them groceries, or paying for some work to be done on their home that you know they cannot afford."
>
> —Chris Gordon[9]

7. Why do women today struggle to feel this loved by God?

8. How does knowing you are this loved impact how you love...
   Your family?

   Your neighbors or coworkers?

   Your least favorite person?

9. Is there a woman in your community you have written off? How can you reach out to her?

Surprised that such a "fairytale" is true? Can a cynical woman of the 21st century actually believe she can be part of this real "Cinderella story"? Sure! Remember, God is the Inventor of "happily ever after." The love He has for us cannot be stopped or lost or thwarted. As determined as Boaz was to marry Ruth, Jesus is even more determined to marry us. And, where we face empty spaces and lost dreams and need a rescue, we can be as confident in Jesus as Naomi was confident in Boaz, because Jesus is a *determined* Redeemer with His eye on us (Rom. 8:31-39).

10. How did history prove that Ruth, an outsider, would become the ultimate insider?

11. How will God work the same kind of inclusion for you over time while you are living? How will He after He sets up the new heavens and new earth?

> "Remembering in community means that we get to witness the before and after transformations of others and the already and not yet journeys we all go through in life. We remember these stories with and for one another. This is necessary because we are prone to remembering selectively, with biases and distortions. We are also prone to forgetfulness."
>
> —Alice Kim[10]

Memory Verse

Once God has spoken; twice have I heard this: that power belongs to God, and that to you, O Lord, belongs steadfast love (Ps. 62:11-12a).

[1] Mike Emlet, "Love Is Inconvenient," *CCEF* (blog), July 30, 2020, https://www.ccef.org/love-is-inconvenient/.

[2] Tony Merida, "Why Hospitality is Vital to Church Planting," *The Gospel Coalition* (blog), February 13, 2018, https://www.thegospelcoalition.org/article/hospitality-vital-church-planting/.

[3] Prasanta Verma, "A Country With No Name: Living in Liminal Spaces," *Asian American Christian Collaborative* (blog), March 23, 2021, https://www.asianamericanchristiancollaborative.com/article/a-country-with-no-name-living-in-liminal-spaces.

[4] Evelyn Simpson-Curenton, "Changed Mah Name," *Lead Me Guide Me Hymnal* (Chicago, IL: GIA Publications, 1987), 275.

[5] Trevin Wax, "How 'Insider/Outsider' Distinctions Inflame Our Devotion," *The Gospel Coalition* (blog), March 2, 2010, https://www.thegospelcoalition.org/blogs/trevin-wax/how-insideroutsider-distinctions-inflame-our-devotion/.

[6] Lori Sealy, "God's Omniscient Wisdom in Our Wilderness Wanderings," *enCourage* (blog), July 29, 2019, https://encourage.pcacdm.org/2019/07/29/post-template-159/.

[7] Augustine in *Prayers of the Early Church*, edited by J. Manning Potts (Nashville: The Upper Room, 1953), 50.

[8] Darby Strickland, "Rejection," *CCEF* (blog), October 6, 2020, https://www.ccef.org/rejection/.

[9] Chris Gordon, "The Resurrection: A Return on Investment," *enCourage* (blog), April 1, 2021, https://encourage.pcacdm.org/2021/04/01/post-template-213-123/.

[10] Alice Kim, "Remembering in Community," *enCourage* (blog), September 28, 2020, https://encourage.pcacdm.org/2020/09/28/post-template-213-66/.

Notes

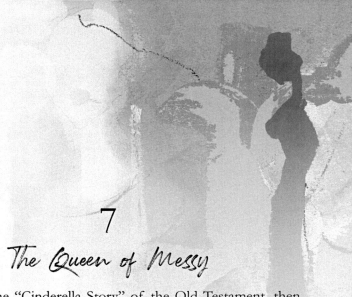

7
The Queen of Messy

If Ruth's is the "Cinderella Story" of the Old Testament, then Bathsheba's gives us one that looks more like a cable news story than a Sunday school story. Are we shocked this story is included in the Bible? Actually, this one-night affair between Israel's King David and the wife of Uriah the Hittite is evidence that the Bible is reliable. Why would any religion include such a moral disaster of one of its best heroes unless it *had* happened this way? And why would God introduce His Son by including Bathsheba? "The wife of Uriah the Hittite" sticks out like a sore thumb in Matthew's genealogy. Bathsheba is tied forever to a sex scandal and murder cover-up, and therefore, so is Jesus.

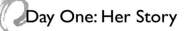

Day One: Her Story

Read 2 Samuel 11-12.

1. Name the outward progression of sin you see in 2 Samuel 11.
   - Verse 1:
   - Verse 2:
   - Verse 3:
   - Verse 4:
   - Verses 6-13:
   - Verses 14-15:

2. How is Nathan's version (2 Samuel 12) of David and Bathsheba's affair different than the narrator's version in 2 Samuel 11?

> "When we are sinned against, we don't confess sinful acts done against us, but death has come close and leaves us connected to the vile actions of others. We need disconnection from sin's power, cleansing and connection to the right person."
>
> —Ed Welch[1]

As we watch David blowing through the commandments regarding coveting, adultery, and murder, Bathsheba almost seems a two-dimensional character without much say. When David called, was she flattered? Scared? Taken aback? After all, her husband Uriah was one of David's band of brothers (2 Sam. 23:39). Later, when she got the death telegram from the war department, did she wonder out loud if it was David's doing? Although David should not have been on the roof skipping his duties as king, did she wonder if she had been responsible for the affair by bathing that night? And, although we do not know what happened behind closed doors, we do see David misused his position of power to sleep with this beautiful woman. Secondly, he betrayed a good friend by ordering his death by war. Lastly, he married Bathsheba and kept on going as if nothing had happened.

And then Nathan showed up.

3. According to Nathan (12:1-9), list several ways David's sin was particularly offensive.

Bible Lagniappe
Swapping Shame for Beauty

One of the consequences of David's sin against God was that his family would be in future turmoil. A particularly heartbreaking account of violence within his family comes in the following chapter, 2 Samuel 13. David's son Ammon rapes his half-sister, David's daughter Tamar (not to be confused with the Tamar of Lesson 3). Moses Y. Lee writes beautifully on how our Heavenly King takes away the shame that Tamar's own daddy-king did not:

> When Tamar cries, 'Where could I carry my shame?' (v. 13), our heavenly Father responds with good news of a future messianic king. God hears Tamar and answers her cry as her rapist brother dismisses it and as her own father, King David, ignores and minimizes it (v. 21). But whereas Tamar put ashes on her head, tore her decorative robe, and waited for the true and better king to carry out justice and restore her stolen dignity, we now have access to Jesus Christ, the king for whom Tamar and those like her have longed.
>
> Only this king compassionately carried all our shame to a cross and died so we could be cleansed of our perpetrators' sins against us and forgiven of the many sins we've committed against others. And only this king rose from the dead to replace our tattered robes by clothing us with his garment of praise, replacing our ashes by covering us with his beauty (Isa. 61:3). In Jesus, our shame, doubts, and false accusations are redeemed and vindicated.[2]

4. List the consequences of David's sin.

5. What was David's response (12:13)?

6. Imagine you are in Bathsheba's shoes during this time. How would you feel about . . .
   Nathan?

   Your baby dying?

   David?

   Yourself?

7. How do women today struggle with guilt of past sins (whether sins they have committed or that have been committed against them)?

Day Two: God's Story

Read 2 Samuel 12 again.

1. Would you describe God sending Nathan to David as a guilt trip or a gift? Why?

2. God used prophets like Nathan to give His people His word. How do you generally respond to correction from God's Word, whether in the form of teaching, preaching, one-on-one conversations, or reading the Bible?

David got away with murder. Literally. The writer doesn't elaborate but almost uncomfortably gives us what we need to know in 2 Samuel 11: a hero's funeral, a quick wedding, and a less-than-nine-months pregnancy. Bathsheba's world may have drastically changed in that year, but David's court seemed to hum along, absorbing one more wife and perhaps one more rumor. Yet, because David was the king—a representative and leader of God's people—we hold our breath because we know God loved His son David and His people too much to let this sin go unaddressed.

> "If God's Word becomes simply one of our options, then we cease to be His servants."
>
> —Dale Ralph Davis[3]

God sent Nathan to court to give David a gift in the form of the story: a story of a poor family with a beloved pet, a story of a mean, rich neighbor who takes their pet for his dinner. We are sickened by the allegory, and David was too. He proclaimed fiery justice. But then Nathan responded, *"You* are the man, David!" and busted wide open the Davidic Cover-Up.

3. Name the people hurt by David's sins.

4. According to 2 Samuel 12:7-12, how did David's sin hurt the LORD?

5. When you sin, name the potential victims of your sins.

6. Why do you think David repented primarily to God, and how does this impact how you view your sins?

> "There's something good in our desire for 'authenticity.' We're tired of masks, and we want to get real. But what if 'authenticity' has become just another mask—one more covering for our sins? While the world tells me to seek its validation for my authentic self, the gospel tells me to seek Jesus's forgiveness for my inexcusable sins. There's a big difference."
> —Emma Scrivener[4]

David felt the deep cut of conviction when Nathan spoke God's word to him. (Prophets such as Nathan were walking "Bibles" to God's people.) As painful as that conviction was, it was the needed first step to restoring David's relationship with God. Today, God's Word continues to hurt, with that good kind of pain, like antiseptic cleaning a festering wound. Ephesians 6:17 calls God's Word "the sword of the Spirit," and it is not a child's toy sword but a sharp, spiritual one. The writer of Hebrews says the Word is "living and active, sharper than any two-edged sword, piercing to the division of soul and of spirit, of joints and of marrow, and discerning the thoughts and intentions of the heart"

(Heb. 4:12). Only God can wield it to target the heart's strongholds of pride, jealousy, discontentment, bitterness, and the sins we can cover up well with good deeds and the privacy allowed by power.

7. How are your sins impacting your relationship with God today?

8. Who (or what) are the "Nathans" in your life and how do you respond to correction?

Psalm 51

Have mercy on me, O God,
   according to your steadfast love;
according to your abundant mercy
   blot out my transgressions.
² Wash me thoroughly from my iniquity,
   and cleanse me from my sin!
³ For I know my transgressions,
   and my sin is ever before me.
⁴ Against you, you only, have I sinned
   and done what is evil in your sight,
so that you may be justified in your words
   and blameless in your judgment.
⁵ Behold, I was brought forth in iniquity,
   and in sin did my mother conceive me.
⁶ Behold, you delight in truth in the inward being,
   and you teach me wisdom in the secret heart.

> [7] *Purge me with hyssop, and I shall be clean;*
> *wash me, and I shall be whiter than snow.*
> [8] *Let me hear joy and gladness;*
> *let the bones that you have broken rejoice.*
> [9] *Hide your face from my sins,*
> *and blot out all my iniquities.*
> [10] *Create in me a clean heart, O God,*
> *and renew a right spirit within me.*
> [11] *Cast me not away from your presence,*
> *and take not your Holy Spirit from me.*
> [12] *Restore to me the joy of your salvation,*
> *and uphold me with a willing spirit.*
> [13] *Then I will teach transgressors your ways,*
> *and sinners will return to you.*
> [14] *Deliver me from bloodguiltiness, O God,*
> *O God of my salvation,*
> *and my tongue will sing aloud of your righteousness.*
> [15] *O Lord, open my lips,*
> *and my mouth will declare your praise.*
> [16] *For you will not delight in sacrifice, or I would give it;*
> *you will not be pleased with a burnt offering.*
> [17] *The sacrifices of God are a broken spirit;*
> *a broken and contrite heart, O God, you will not despise.*
> [18] *Do good to Zion in your good pleasure;*
> *build up the walls of Jerusalem;*
> [19] *then will you delight in right sacrifices,*
> *in burnt offerings and whole burnt offerings;*
> *then bulls will be offered on your altar.*

9. Think of a sin you've committed. Use David's confession to help with your own. (David penned Psalm 51 after the events of 2 Samuel 11 & 12.)
    - Verses 1-4
    David's confession:

    Your confession:

- Verses 5-9
  David's confession:

  Your confession:

- Verses 10-14
  David's confession:

  Your confession:

- Verses 14-17
  David's confession:

  Your confession:

- Verses 18-19
  David's confession:

  Your confession:

How does this story end? God accepted David's confession, quickly and fully. The sweet words of Nathan, "The LORD also has put away your sin" (12:13) rang out in the room. While David and his family would live with the consequences of his sins, the relationship and promises David had with God were not wiped out. As a "man after God's own heart" (Acts 13:22), imagine David's relief, hope, and thankfulness.

The forgiveness David received was also a mercy for his people. As the ruling head of Israel, David needed to be right with God in order to guide and lead them. After years and years of good and bad kings (and David was actually one of the stellar ones), we will see that no mere man could be a perfect king, the kind of king God's people really needed. The Gospel of Matthew introduces us to the One who is. Jesus is the King who fully obeyed in all the places David and his descendants did not.

Bible Lagniappe
Sing Like You're Forgiven

As a little girl I heard snippets of Paul Harvey's radio program "The Rest of the Story." In a way, we get to see the rest of this story unfold in subsequent chapters of 2 Samuel, and we see what Nathan alluded to when he spoke about the consequences for shaming God's name (2 Sam. 12:10). As David wrote psalms based on his life, Psalm 3 reflects what he is feeling during one of these hard consequences. David and his tattered band of women, children, and a few followers are escaping his son Absalom's coup. Although David was reaping what he sowed in 2 Samuel 11, David sings this song like one forgiven and restored. He is confident of God's love and protection as his personal, covenant God even as he walked the path of suffering due to his and others' sins.

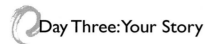# Day Three: Your Story

How do you think Bathsheba felt marrying the man who killed her husband? Imagine her complicated emotions. Did she feel shame or guilt? Many women today struggle with guilt over things they did in their past, everything from a betrayal of a good friend in high school to an abortion no one knows about. Or they have survived sins of others such as abuse, neglect, and racist jabs. The shame or guilt can stick to us women, and Bathsheba would understand. In a one night stand, her life turned upside down. Was she ever able to move past it?

Read 2 Samuel 12:16-25.

1. Why did David fast and pray?

2. Why did the baby die? How do you feel about his death?

3. After David's baby died, what did David do, and why?

4. In Psalm 3, we see how David prayed when facing one of the consequences of this sin. Compare Psalm 3 and 2 Samuel 12:20-23. List ways he demonstrated he felt forgiven.

Experiencing every parent's nightmare, Bathsheba watched her son die. Did her memories of the night with David haunt her as they buried their child? An empty baby bed mocked her more than any court rumor would have. Her messy life careened into grief.

Yet when God forgave David, He did not forgive in a stingy way, nor did He forget Bathsheba in His forgiveness. Notice in 2 Samuel 12:24, the writer begins to call her by her name, Bathsheba, not "the wife of Uriah." Her identity is no longer associated with "That Sin" but with the future—with a baby. Many times, sins like these wreck a family, but we see the fruits of true repentance and forgiveness. First, David comforted Bathsheba's sadness, preventing the dark isolation of shame. Then, God gave them another baby boy, Solomon, meaning "peace" or "replacement."[5] Instead of confrontation, the same prophet Nathan brought news that God loved this baby. God did not take away the promises to David that his descendant will sit on this throne. Bathsheba called her son Jedidiah, "beloved of the LORD."[6]

Imagine the difference in Bathsheba and David. They looked at this boy and saw God's pleasure, delight, and continuing covenant love. They saw their future tied to this merciful God and not tied up in shame. As awful as the consequences would be for David and his family, the worst thing did not happen. God did not abandon him nor His promise that David's Son (Luke 18:38) would eternally rule.

5. Name consequences of sins that women live with today.

6. Explain the difference between God's judgment on sin and the consequences of sins in your life.

7. According to these passages, how does God forgive your sins?

- Psalm 32:5

- Psalm 103:12

- Isaiah 1:18

- Isaiah 55:7

- Acts 3:19

- Ephesians 1:7

8. What does it look like when women live in light of God's forgiveness instead of in the shadow of guilt?

Sexual sins are extremely hard to forget, whether you are to blame or not. Women carry scars from others' abuse, their own dumb decisions, or rebellious lifestyles. The church should be the first place these women go for safety, comfort, and support for getting beyond their guilt. However, instead of offering the hand of grace and mercy, many Christians have looked at struggling women with disdain or awkwardness. We do not see how a woman who aborted her child can become "beloved of the LORD," or we do not see how a woman struggling with same-sex attraction can be spiritually kin to God's people. We condemn her based on our own rules instead of include her based on Jesus's mercy, "Let him who is without sin among you be the first to throw a stone at her" (John 8:7).

Or our sins shout louder than Jesus's words of forgiveness, and we isolate from Christian community feeling unlovable, exposed, vulnerable to more hurt over a dirty past. Jesus never covers up our sin by saying they did not happen or letting us ignore them. He actually sees our sins and yucky lives more clearly than we do. And, like a Big Brother getting His little sister out of jail, he counts out the whole payment to free her. Every. Little. Bit. And the currency He used was His own blood. It's the only currency that spends in Heaven. Then, when He takes us out of our prisons of guilt and shame, He looks at us and our churches saying, "Therefore I tell you, her sins, which are many, are forgiven" (Luke 7:47).

9. What has He fully forgiven you of today?

10. How do you look at forgiven women today?

> "I bring my heart to you, Lord, because I know that I'm proud and stubborn. And as much as I hate the consequences of this sin, I don't want to give it up. So, there . . . I said it. I hate it, and I love it. I hate feeling guilty, like a bad Christian. The mental assault of all that I've stockpiled in my mind from having this sin control me for so long is torment. However, I love escaping the stress of my life for a few minutes or hours; I like the intoxicating pleasure I get. I know it's wrong, but it feels good. Why does it have to be that way, Lord? That sin feels good and life-giving, while obedience can feel boring, painful, and deathly? Why?! (Ps. 51:1-2)."
>
> —Ellen Dykas[7]

Memory Verse

**Create in me a clean heart, O God,
 and renew a right spirit within me (Ps. 51:10).**

---

[1] Ed Welch, "The Gospel for Shame," *CCEF* (blog), June 26, 2018, https://www.ccef.org/shame/.

[2] Moses Y. Lee, "The Cruelty of Victim-Blaming and the Hope for Redemption," *The Gospel Coalition* (blog), October 22, 2018, https://www.thegospelcoalition.org/article/cruelty-victim-blaming-hope-redemption/.

[3] Dale Ralph Davis, used with written permission by the author.

[4] Emma Scrivener, "The Problem with Authenticity," *The Gospel Coalition* (blog), September 7, 2017, https://www.thegospelcoalition.org/article/the-problem-with-authenticity/.

[5] Commentary on 2 Samuel 12:24, *The Reformation Study Bible* (Philipsburg, NJ: P & R Publishing, 2008), 443.

[6] Ibid., Note on v. 25.

[7] Ellen Dykas, "A Fresh Start in Battling Sin," *Harvest USA* (blog), January 7, 2021, https://harvestusa.org/a-prayer-for-a-fresh-start-in-battling-sin/#.YGYLwR1Ol-U.

Notes

8
The Unwed Teenage Mother

Congrats! It's a boy!

Luke's gospel opens with a strange baby announcement. Gabriel (one of God's top angels) visited two servants of God, telling them they would be having special babies. The fact that the mothers-to-be were either barren or a virgin does not seem to matter. As the archangel said, "with God nothing will be impossible" (Luke 1:37 NKJV).

Day One: Her Story

Read Luke 1:1-38.

1. Contrast Zechariah's response to Gabriel (1:18) with Mary's response to Gabriel (1:34).

2. How fully do you think Mary understood God's answer to her question in 1:34-37?

3. Name some things God is doing in your life that you do not quite fully understand.

Usually, the parents get to announce they are expecting a baby. But what happens when you are expecting the Messiah? A book for new parents called *What to Expect When You're Expecting the Messiah* did not exist to guide Mary and Joseph. Not only was the birth announcement odd, but who would have guessed a nobody from Nazareth would carry The Baby, the answer to all of Israel's hopes and prayers. Reminiscent of Mt. Carmel (1 Kings 18) when Elijah doused the wood with water before God lit it on fire to prove His power, Mary's pregnancy seemed just as an unlikely and crazy way to show off His power and purposes of redemption.

Meanwhile, the priest Zechariah was just as flabbergasted with Gabriel's news as Mary was, yet his response earned an archangel's rebuke. Zechariah responded with "How will I know?" The more experienced "church worker" lost sight of *Who* was sending this unlikely word. Mary, although young and inexperienced, had questions but did not question God Himself. Although women today may not have Gabriel as a drop-by guest, many promises for us from God's Word seem impossible.

> "Friends, what did we sign up for when we became followers of Jesus? Or asking it another way, what did we understand the Christian life to entail once we believed, committed, and began to follow Jesus? Were you told that Jesus blesses his followers with abundance and ease as a reward for forsaking sin, especially the ones we most enjoy? Maybe like many of us, you just assumed that a loving, gracious God would remove troubles, because after all, he has the power to do so!"
>
> —Ellen Dykas[1]

4. What are the impossible things God is calling you to believe today?

5. Name ways you can imitate Mary's response of humble obedience in how you respond to God's call on your life.

Like He did with Mary, God asks us to trust and obey Him even when we do not understand how He will make it happen. This kind of situation may look like an unexplainable peace in a cancer ward, the confidence to confront a close friend, or the ability to snuggle someone else's baby after your miscarriage. Those are impossible things to do on your own. The only way they happen is when Jesus's Spirit enlarges your heart to do them (Ps. 119:32). When faced with the impossible, we must repeat Mary's words—"Behold, the maidservant of the LORD"—and remember the truth of Gabriel's "nothing is impossible with God."

> "You don't have to understand things for them to be."
> —Madeline L'Engle[2]

Day Two: God's Story

Imagine how shocked Mary was when Gabriel interrupted her day. Although she had grown up with the prophecies of "Immanuel, God with us" (Isa. 7:14), she probably never dreamed her story would intersect in such a specific way with The Story.

CHARLIE BROWN: I guess you were right, Linus. I shouldn't have picked this little tree. Everything I do turns into a disaster. I guess I don't really know what Christmas is all about. (*unhinged*) Isn't there anyone who knows what Christmas is all about?"

LINUS: Sure, Charlie Brown, I can tell you what Christmas is all about.

Linus walks to center stage, dragging his blanket.

LINUS: Lights, please?

Auditorium lights dim and spot shines on Linus.

LINUS: "And there were in the same country shepherds abiding in the field, keeping watch over their flock by night. And, lo, the angel of the Lord came upon them, and the glory of the Lord shone round about them. And they were sore afraid. And the angel said unto them, "Fear not, for behold, I bring you good tidings of great joy, which shall be to all people. For unto you is born this day in the city of David a Saviour, which is Christ the Lord..."[3]

1. This birth announcement was centuries in the making. Trace the clues in the following passages:

- Genesis 3:15

- Isaiah 7:14

- Matthew 1:18-25

- Galatians 4:4-5

2. According to Galatians 4:4-5, why did this pregnancy have to happen "now"?

I can only imagine how excited Heaven was when Gabriel left to deliver his message to Mary. Just like a woman who feels she's about to pop with a full-term pregnancy, Heaven must have been about to pop when the time came, and God cued the heavenly choir above the shepherds (Luke 2). After all, Peter later wrote that "even angels long to look into these things" (1 Peter 1:12) when it comes to how God saves us. The birth of Jesus is when God's Big Story gets very tangible. For centuries God's people had waited on Him to keep the promises He had made to Adam and Eve in Eden (Gen. 3:15). If you have a Bible timeline, you can trace all the snapshots of salvation He gave Noah, Abraham, Moses, and David. These promises revealed more and more what God was doing to get us back in relationship with Him. Like sonogram photos parents show their friends, God gave His people pictures of the kind of salvation He had in mind. When Jeremiah 31 says that the old covenant and its laws were obsolete, it is like saying, "The baby is coming!" Fast forward to the New Testament, and we see the writer of Hebrews telling his readers, don't go back to the sonograms! They are obsolete now that the baby is here. Embrace Jesus, He is better than all the ceremonies and special holidays you had before. After all, no parent shows off sonograms once the baby has arrived!

3. Compare the prophecies of the Old Testament (below) with the story of Jesus's life.

Prophecy	Fulfillment
2 Sam. 7:16	Luke 4:16
Isa. 7:14	Luke 1
Gen. 3:15	Acts 2:31
Micah 5:2	Luke 2:4
Hosea 11:1	Matt. 2:19-21
Ps. 22	Luke 24:25-26

By the end of Luke's book, we see Jesus walking along the road to Emmaus with two friends explaining how the Old Testament had been pointing to Him all along (Luke 24:13-27). The ceremonial sacrifices of Moses's day had pointed to a need for the shedding of blood. The sufferings of the prophets had hinted that Jesus would suffer, too. God's people would have a King not for earthly victories, but for the larger victories over sin and death.

> ### *Bible Lagniappe*
> ### What's the Shekinah Glory?
>
> In the Old Testament days, the people saw a cloud by day and a fire by night to signal He was "home" with them, in His tent or tabernacle. Later, this Shekinah Glory filled the temple Solomon built. But, as God's people continued to disobey Him, His prophet Ezekiel tells them God would withdraw His presence from them. You can trace this Shekinah Glory leaving the temple in Ezekiel 10. But, in Luke 2:9, we see that Shekinah Glory come back when the angel appears to the shepherds, announcing Jesus's birth! God sent His only Son to live among His people and pay the price for our sins, so we can never experience the absence of His presence again.

4. Knowing how God unfolded His Big Story, how will you read the Bible differently?

5. When you are overwhelmed with anything from the mess in your world to the mess of your weekly calendar, how can God's story of redemption comfort you?

Come, Thou Long-Expected Jesus[4]

Come, thou long expected Jesus,
born to set thy people free;
from our fears and sins release us,
let us find our rest in thee.
Israel's strength and consolation,
hope of all the earth thou art;
dear desire of every nation,
joy of every longing heart.

Born thy people to deliver,
born a child and yet a King,
born to reign in us forever,
now thy gracious kingdom bring.
By thine own eternal spirit
rule in all our hearts alone;
by thine all sufficient merit,
raise us to thy glorious throne.

Day Three: Your Story

Read Luke 1:35-38.

Mary had a great future. She was engaged to a wonderful guy. Perhaps Mary was flipping through bridal magazines or making a wedding invitation list when Gabriel busted in. Then, just one angel visit later, her life was turned upside down. For a "good Jewish girl," getting pregnant out of wedlock was shocking. Joseph, her fiancé, did not buy her Gabriel narrative and made plans to call off their wedding once he heard she was pregnant (Matt. 1:18-21). Not a very good start when she was only living out God's plan.

1. Can you name times that your plans were changed by circumstances outside your control?

2. How do you view God when your plans get changed?

> "Sometimes when we say 'God is silent,' what's really going on is that he hasn't told the story the way we wanted it told. He will be silent when we want him to fill in the blanks of the story we are creating. But with his own stories, the ones we live in, he is seldom silent."
> —Paul E. Miller[5]

3. Imagine you are in Mary's shoes. How would you feel?

Mary's life as mother to Jesus was special, but it was not especially easy. Where was Gabriel when they wandered door to door looking for a place to deliver this Baby? Was she questioning God's plan when she saw the Jewish rulers attack Jesus? Did her faith quiver as she heard of His arrest? From fleeing Herod's murder of Bethlehem boys to seeing her grown Son die on a cross, Mary's life was one heartbreak after another (Luke 2:35).

> "Never be afraid to trust an unknown future to a known God."
> —Corrie ten Boom[6]

4. When obedience to God's commands brings heartache and difficulty, how do you typically respond?

5. Notice how Mary responded to news of her upcoming pregnancy. How can you do the same when God throws you a "curve ball"?

	Mary's response	Your response
Luke 1:38a		
Luke 1:38b		
Luke 1:39		

Although Mary was young (possibly even 13 or 14), her response to Gabriel teaches us how to accept the hardships we encounter. Mary said she would do whatever God asked of her (Luke 1:38). Although she could not picture where this path of obedience would take her, she submitted to whatever it was because God was trustworthy. But what did she do after that? First, she sought encouragement from someone who would understand her unusual pregnancy, her cousin Elizabeth (1:39-45). Elizabeth blessed her for believing (1:45). Here was one family member who believed her story! But that is not the last we hear of Mary's life with an unexpected pregnancy. Later, when the shepherds barged into her barnyard childbirth suite, she pondered what God was doing (2:19). And probably there were days she just did not understand what was happening (Luke 2:50).

> "When we tell people God will never give them more than they can handle, we are ultimately saying they are stronger than they think they are. The truth of the matter is that you and I are much weaker than we like to believe. But praise be to God, he is bigger and stronger and wiser and kinder than we can ever imagine."
>
> —Courtney Doctor[7]

We will not have Mary's particular burden of mothering the Messiah, but we will have difficult stories. From widespread catastrophes like a hurricane to the individual catastrophes of losing a family member, suffering is part of our lives.

6. What do the following passages teach God's followers about suffering?
   - Psalm 34:19

   - Psalm 56:8

   - Isaiah 43:2

   - Romans 5:3-4

   - 2 Corinthians 4:16-18

   - Philippians 3:7-11

   - James 1:12

   - 1 Peter 5:10

> "Pain insists upon being attended to. God whispers to us in our pleasures...but shouts to us in our pain. It is his megaphone to rouse a deaf world."
> —C.S. Lewis[8]

7. Look up Hebrews 2:18. How does it help you to know Jesus understands your pain in suffering?

Unuttered Prayer[9]

My God, sometimes I cannot pray,
Nor can I tell why thus I weep;
The words my heart has framed I cannot say,
Behold me prostrate at Thy feet.

Thou understandest all my woe;
Thou know'st the craving of my soul—
Thine eye beholdeth wheresoe'er I go;
Thou canst this wounded heart make whole.

And oh! while prostrate here I lie,
And groan the words I fain would speak:
Unworthy though I be, pass not me by,
But let Thy love in showers break.

And deluge all my thirsty soul,
And lay my proud ambition low;
So while time's billows o'er me roll,
I shall be washed as white as snow.

Thou wilt not quench the smoking flax,
Nor wilt thou break the bruised reed;
Like potter's clay, or molten wax,
Mould me to suit Thy will indeed.

Paul tells us in Romans 8:28, that all things—including the hospice rooms, unfair office dynamics, and all the skinned knees of parenting—work together for good. This is a stabilizing force when we ask God like Mary did, "How can this be?"

And, echoing Gabriel's words back to Mary, Jesus answers, "With man this is impossible, but with God all things are possible" (Matt. 19:26).

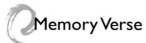
Memory Verse

Trust in the LORD with all your heart, and do not lean on your own understanding (Prov. 3:5).

---

[1] Ellen Dykas, "I Didn't Sign Up for This!" *enCourage* (blog), March 18, 2021, https://encourage.pcacdm.org/2021/03/18/post-template-213-117/.

[2] Madeline L'Engle, *A Wrinkle in Time* (New York, NY: Random House, Inc., 1962), 23.

[3] Lee Mendelson, *A Charlie Brown Christmas: The Making of a Tradition* (New York: Harper Collins, 2000), 175-177.

[4] Charles Wesley, "Come, Thou Long-Expected Jesus," *Trinity Hymnal* (Suwanee, GA: Great Commission Publications, 2018), 196.

[5] Paul E. Miller, *A Praying Life: Connecting with God in a Distracting World* (Colorado Springs, CO: NavPress, 2017), 203.

[6] Corrie ten Boom. Used with permission from the Corrie ten Boom House Foundation, Haarlem, Holland.

[7] Courtney Doctor, "We Can't Handle It," *enCourage* (blog), February 20, 2017, http://encourage.pcacdm.org/2017/02/20/we-cant-handle-it/.

[8] C.S. Lewis, *The Problem of Pain* (San Francisco: HarperSanFrancisco, 2001), 91.

[9] Josephine Heard, "Unuttered Prayer" in *Conversations with God: Two Centuries of Prayers by African Americans*, ed., James Melvin Washington, PhD (New York, NY: HarperCollins, 1994), 65.

Notes

9
Magnificat!

What did Mary do when she found herself expecting the Messiah? She took a trip to her cousin Elizabeth's. (We met her husband, Zechariah, in the last chapter.) As only two women could do, they immediately started talking with excitement, but it was about more than decorating baby nurseries. They saw their God at work using their individual circumstances to accomplish salvation on a massive scale. Elizabeth encouraged Mary by saying she was blessed because she believed God and that God would keep His word. In other words, Mary was not crazy to believe this unbelievable story.

In response, Mary broke out into song. Not only did Mary and Elizabeth have a duet moment of praise over their babies, but we also get to join in Mary's song today. This young girl's story teaches the world about the Lord and how He works.

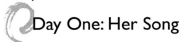
Day One: Her Song

Read Luke 1:46-55.

1. Google or grab a dictionary and find *magnificat*. What is the definition?

2. Name specific things Mary mentioned as she praised God.
   - Verses 46-48: God is...

   - Verse 49: God is...

   - Verse 50: God is...

   - Verse 51: God is...

   - Verse 52: God is...

   - Verse 53: God is...

   - Verses 54-55: God is...

3. How did Mary see her pregnancy connected to the patriarch Abraham?

4. Describe what "proud in the thoughts of their hearts" (1:51b) looks like today.

5. Why did Mary express her thoughts in a song?

Sometimes things are just too big to contain. When Mary arrived at Elizabeth's house, their moment in history was just too big for a simple cousin hug. They all (including the unborn John the Baptist jumping for joy in utero) recognized something glorious was happening. Only a song would do. And, how good of God to give us this song to sing along with her.

Mary started her song with a "bang"—"My soul magnifies the Lord"—and continued with wonder that her poverty and insignificance did not stop God from picking her to be part of this Story. She may have been young, inexperienced, and small, but her big God "has done great things for [her]" (v. 49). His love for her was personal, but Mary's words go beyond her joy of God seeing her and putting her on the front row. She sang in "scripturese" to celebrate how God was working on a grander, more magnificent scale, too. She understood the connection between her story and The Story as she described what kind of God her God is. Was she picturing the Red Sea parting as she sang of His power? Did she think back to the stories she had heard of manna and of the rock pouring out water in the wilderness of His mercy? Was she amazed at His loyalty, relieved that her people's many rebellions had not run God off for good? This unknown girl, centuries from the flashy moments of Israel's past, connected God's covenant kindness to her with God's promises to Abraham!

6. You may not actually sing out loud, but if you were to write a song about God's power, mercy, and loyal love in your life, what would you want to include in your stanzas?

I've Got a Robe
(Going to Shout All Over God's Heaven)[1]

I've got a robe, you've got a robe
All of God's children got a robe
When I get to Heaven goin' to put on my robe
Goin' to shout all over God's Heaven

Heav'n, Heav'n
Ev'rybody talkin' 'bout Heav'n ain't goin' there
Heav'n, Heav'n
Goin' to shout all over God's Heaven

I've got a crown, you've got a crown
All of God's children got a crown
When I get to Heaven goin' to put on my crown
Goin' to shout over God's Heaven

I've got shoes, you've got a shoes
All of God's children got shoes
When I get to Heaven goin' to put on my shoes
Goin' to walk all over God's Heaven

> I've got a harp, you've got a harp
> All of God's children got a harp
> When I get to Heaven goin' to play on my harp
> Goin' to play all over God's Heaven
>
> I've got a song, you've got a song
> All of God's children got a song
> When I get to Heaven goin' to sing a new song
> Goin' to sing all over God's Heaven

Day Two: God's Song

Mary is not the only one who has sung a song of covenant love. God Himself sings over us (Zeph. 3:17).

1. Read Zephaniah 3:14-20 below. Circle or highlight phrases that remind you of Mary's song.

¹⁴ Sing aloud, O daughter of Zion;
   shout, O Israel!
Rejoice and exult with all your heart,
   O daughter of Jerusalem!
¹⁵ The LORD has taken away the judgments against you;
   he has cleared away your enemies.
The King of Israel, the LORD, is in your midst;
   you shall never again fear evil.
¹⁶ On that day it shall be said to Jerusalem:
"Fear not, O Zion;
   let not your hands grow weak.
¹⁷ The LORD your God is in your midst,
   a mighty one who will save;
he will rejoice over you with gladness;
   he will quiet you by his love;
he will exult over you with loud singing.
¹⁸ I will gather those of you who mourn for the festival,
   so that you will no longer suffer reproach.
¹⁹ Behold, at that time I will deal
   with all your oppressors.
And I will save the lame

>   and gather the outcast,
> and I will change their shame into praise
>   and renown in all the earth.
> [20] At that time I will bring you in,
>   at the time when I gather you together;
> for I will make you renowned and praised
>   among all the peoples of the earth,
> when I restore your fortunes
>   before your eyes," says the LORD.

Mary's song reflects God's greater song throughout the Bible, a song of God's love for His people. More tender than a mother's lullaby is this song God Himself sings over His children. Just as a mother smooths her baby's furrowed brow, so God soothes away our judgments and guilt. We relax as our God, like a Mama Bear, chases off our fears as well as our taunting enemies of shame, leaving us at peace in His arms. And, only as a doting parent can call an ugly child beautiful, He sees us in the righteousness of Christ (Zech. 3:4) and adores us.

2. Review the other women we have studied. Give specific examples of how these women could have sung along with Mary about God's faithfulness in their stories:

   Tamar

   Rahab

   Ruth

   Bathsheba

3. Give specific examples from your life of how you can sing along with Mary.

4. Look up the following passages and write down how God works. Do you see any trends?

   1 Kings 17:8-15

   2 Kings 5

   Zechariah 4:5-10

   Matthew 13:31-32

   Luke 18:15-17

   John 6:1-14

Mary's song also reflects how God loves us by using the small to accomplish the big. Hannah sang a similar song in 1 Samuel 2 when she praised God for upending the proud and raising the humble. Jesus's Sermon on the Mount, including the Beatitudes (Matt. 5:1-11), introduces the economy of His new kingdom which is opposite of the world's. In God's kingdom the small of the world are big. The poor in spirit are blessed, not the proud. The meek will win, not the brash and powerful. The ones who suffer now will be joyful in the end. And, with a twist of irony, the death of Mary's baby will deal the blow to Death itself (Heb. 2:14).

God delights in showing off when He uses the smallest and weakest tools to do His work. He even uses things that do not make sense (for example, the ostrich in Job 39:13-18). Just looking back over the Old Testament, we see this in living color as we walk along with broken men and women used to communicate how great and powerful God is. Parables and miracles of the New Testament illustrate this same God is continuing to do His work as He uses a ragamuffin group of followers to bring down Satan from his perch of power (Luke 10:18).

> **A Fire Is Started in Bethlehem**[2]
>
> In a cold and humble stable,
> Blooms a spotless white Carnation,
> That becomes a lovely purple Lily,
> Sacrificed for our redemption.

Bible Lagniappe
Isn't It Ironic?

God delights in using the unusual. In Job 38 and 39, God responds to Job's cries to understand what God is doing in his life. God answers him by listing all the things He created that are past our understanding and ability to control, much less create as He did. My favorite example is the ostrich (Job 39:13-18), a bird that cannot fly and crushes her eggs but can outrun a racehorse. Who would create a bird that can't fly? His ways are just not our ways (Isa. 55:8-10).

---

5. Describe times you have seen God use the messy, the unlikely, or the small things of this world to accomplish His purposes.

Magnificat!

Then Hannah prayed and said:

"My heart rejoices in the LORD;
in the LORD my horn is lifted high.
My mouth boasts over my enemies,
for I delight in your deliverance.
2 "There is no one holy like the LORD;
there is no one besides you;
there is no Rock like our God.
3 "Do not keep talking so proudly
or let your mouth speak such arrogance,
for the LORD is a God who knows,
and by him deeds are weighed.
4 "The bows of the warriors are broken,
but those who stumbled are armed with strength.
5 Those who were full hire themselves out for food,
but those who were hungry are hungry no more.
She who was barren has borne seven children,
but she who has had many sons pines away.
6 "The LORD brings death and makes alive;
he brings down to the grave and raises up.
7 The LORD sends poverty and wealth;
he humbles and he exalts.
8 He raises the poor from the dust
and lifts the needy from the ash heap;
he seats them with princes
and has them inherit a throne of honor.
"For the foundations of the earth are the LORD's;
on them he has set the world.
9 He will guard the feet of his faithful servants,
but the wicked will be silenced in the place of darkness.
"It is not by strength that one prevails;
10 those who oppose the LORD will be broken.
The Most High will thunder from heaven;
the LORD will judge the ends of the earth.
"He will give strength to his king
and exalt the horn of his anointed."

1 Samuel 2:1-10 (NIV)

Day Three: Your Song

Maybe you don't break out in song as Mary did, but does your heart skip a beat as you consider His character, His love for you, His delight in using you in His kingdom, and the part you get to play in His story? As He was for Mary, is Jesus your muse when it comes to your imagination and dreams for this life and the next? Bottom line: are you in love with God?

> "Forgive me for being so ordinary while claiming to know so extraordinary a God."
> —Jim Elliot[3]

Many days we do not feel the warm fuzzies of faith. In those times, looking at God's Word helps your heart see what it may be missing.

1. Go back to question 1 on Day One. Transcribe the list of God's attributes you wrote below that correspond to Mary's song, and then fill in how you see or want to see them in your life today:

Mary's song	Attributes of God	How I see (or need to see) those in my life
1:46-48		
1:49		
1:50		
1:51		
1:52		
1:53		
1:54-55		

2. Name the small things God is using in your life today to encourage you, grow you, or help you.

God was redeeming His creation and an entire people but stooped to care for Mary in such a personal way. He gave her Elizabeth to sing with, to learn from, and to prepare with as they faced the joy and the overwhelming miracles of their pregnancies. This is how God loves, not only in cosmic bold strokes for the world, but in the detailed touches for us individually. Sending the just-right hospice nurse, providing a soothing Bible verse on a difficult day, or causing the budding trees outside your window to proclaim His faithfulness as winter still hangs on are all ways God puts His arms around us. And, as He works our small things together for good, He simultaneously orchestrates a melody of salvation for people over vast times and places. He is unlimited in His abilities, yet attentive to our smallest needs.

3. Name your smallest needs. Then name the big ones.

4. When are times you have felt particularly seen and known by God?

> "God unites people together for all sorts of reasons. He places encouragers to lift us up when we've hit a low point. He rallies champions when we've lost the power to fight another minute. He brings admonishers and counselors to guide us through sticky decisions. He gifts us lovers and friends to sweeten our days with laughter and joy."
>
> —Heather Molendyk[4]

5. Describe how God gave you an "Elizabeth" when you needed her. How can you cultivate the type of relationship Mary and Elizabeth shared?

6. So many women need an "Elizabeth" in their emotional moments of life. How can you, as an individual or your community, intentionally do what Elizabeth did for Mary?

Memory Verse

What then shall we say in response to these things? If God is for us, who can be against us? He who did not spare his own Son but gave him up for us all—how will he not also, along with him, graciously give us all things? (Rom. 8:31-32).

[1] J. Jefferson Cleveland, ed., *Songs of Zion* (Nashville: Abingdon Press, 1981), 82.

[2] Translation of "En Belén Tocan a Fuego," traditional Castilian Carol in *The International Book of Christmas Carols*, edited by Walter Ehret and George K. Evans (Englewood Cliffs, NJ: Prentice-Hall, 1963), 277.

[3] Jim Elliot, *The Journals of Jim Elliot,* edited by Elisabeth Elliot (Grand Rapids, MI: Fleming H. Revel, 1978), 98.

[4] Heather Molendyk, "Covenant Friendships," *enCourage* (blog), October 22, 2020, https://encourage.pcacdm.org/2020/10/22/post-template-213-75/.

Notes

In Closing

Mary's song sums up this study well. Her song reflects a God who uses women such as Tamar, Rahab, Ruth, Bathsheba, and Mary to bring salvation to many. Today women are tempted to think living for God means living large for God, doing something extraordinary. Or in contrast, they believe God only uses "good girls" in His kingdom. Actually, God prefers to use the anonymous and unlikely to accomplish His redemption. Knowing this gives us confidence to go where He sends us, whether to a new city or into a new season of life. His powers enable our small hands and feet to do His big work. And, His loyal love sticks with us, never leaving us alone to face what He puts on our path.

So, if you struggle to be brave enough, remember Mary's song. If you cannot see past your weaknesses, remind yourself that He delights in showing off His power through them (2 Cor. 12:9-10). As you contemplate your small place in the world, fix your eyes on Jesus who connects with all kinds of women. He loved women like the forlorn widow walking behind a coffin (Luke 7:11-17) and the sinful woman washing His feet in front of the church leaders (Luke 7:36-50). His physical touch healed the untouchable bleeding woman as He went to undo the death of a little girl (Luke 8:40-56). His earthly ministry was supported by the likes of Mary Magdalene, previously possessed by seven demons, along with leaders in the community such as Joanna and Susanna (Luke 8:1-3).

If Jesus welcomes all these different kinds of women, should not His people as well? Who are the Tamars in your Sunday school classes? Would a Bathsheba feel welcomed in your neighborhood prayer group? As we encounter outsiders like Ruth or a woman with a past like Rahab, let us see them as Jesus does. Forgiven and loved. Pure and worthy. And, if anyone asks, "What's *she* doing here?" You can answer as Jesus would. She belongs here; she's with me.

Appendix

Leader's Guide for Small Group Discussion

"I don't know" is okay to say.

There's nothing wrong with saying I don't know to someone's question. If you get a question you can't answer on the spot, ask everyone to look into Scripture that week and discuss it later. If you are part of a church, consider asking a staff member for more insight or information. Paul loved how the "noble Bereans" did not just take his word for it, but looked to the Scriptures themselves for truth (Acts 17:11).

Stay off the rabbit trail.

If the group discussion gets on a rabbit trail, steer the group back to the discussion questions saying something like, "Those are great questions, but let's get back to the questions on page 14." However, sometimes the conversation goes to a good place, and you may want to take advantage. God loves to give wisdom (James 1:5), so pray for the wisdom to know when to continue and when to redirect.

Mind your manners.

Some Christians, especially those who have participated in Bible study for years, can come across as a "know-it-all." Encourage a safe atmosphere for the inquiring visitor or new believer. Lead the discussion with your own questions. Do not assume women know where the books of the Bible are without the table of contents. If you feel someone in your group is intimidating others by her strong personality or views, you may want to think about approaching her privately, encouraging her to be thoughtful and "share the mic."

Be aware of advice frenzy.

Remember that our goal is to look at what Scripture has to say, not what each lady's opinion is. If different views of Scripture are brought up by individuals in your group, you may acknowledge that Christians do not always agree on everything the Bible says, but our church teaches _____. Encourage the ladies to look in the Bible themselves to see if their viewpoint is in line with the Scriptures.

Guard your group.

Encourage confidentiality in your prayer group to not share telltale details about someone else's problem. Be thoughtful of their schedules and start and end the group on time. Be sensitive to the different walks and seasons of life in your group, and do not let a majority dominate the conversation. For example, if the young moms in the group take the majority of time comparing dirty diaper tales (a worthy subject), the college student may feel like she does not belong.

Feel free to follow up.

You may pick up on a voice quiver or tears right behind the eyes during a discussion or prayer request. Sending a text, meeting for lunch, or just talking on the way out the door is a good way to provide space for a private conversation. Many women want to talk about an issue but find a group of any size intimidating to bring that topic up whether personal or theological.

Pray.

Ask God to give you insight and wisdom. Pray for the women in your group. Ask your Heavenly Father for a soft heart toward the difficult personalities and a courageous heart when your group is painfully quiet. And when you are discouraged by those who do not complete their discussion questions, by those who cancel at the last minute, or by those who talk too much or too little, remember God never lets His Word return empty (Isa. 55:11). Also, prayer pages follow to help your group members keep up with various prayer requests throughout your time together.

"Is prayer your steering wheel or your spare tire?"
—Corrie ten Boom[1]

Name/Date	Prayer Request

[1] Corrie ten Boom. Used with permission of Corrie Ten Boom House Foundation.

"The great thing in prayer is to feel that we are putting our supplications into the bosom of omnipotent love."
—Andrew Murray[2]

Name/Date	Prayer Request

[2] Andrew Murray, quoted in Daniel Partner. *The One Year Book of Personal Prayer* (Wheaton, IL: Tyndale House, 1991) 264.

> "Prayer is a moment of incarnation—God with us. God involved in the details of my life"
> —Paul Miller[3]

Name/Date	Prayer Request

---

[3] Paul Miller, *A Praying Life: Connecting with God in a Distracting World* (Colorado Springs, CO: NavPress, 2017), 109.

"Where God leads you to pray, He means for you to receive."
—Charles Spurgeon[4]

Name/Date	Prayer Request

[4] C.H. Spurgeon, as quoted by Derek Thomas. *Praying the Saviour's Way* (Fearn Ross-Shire, UK: Christian Focus Publications, 2002), 133.

"Prayer is not just a spiritual discipline, it is the divine safety valve for our fondest hopes and most anxious fears."
—Rondi Lauterback[5]

Name/Date	Prayer Request

[5] Rondi Lauterback, "Prayer and Jesus' Invitation to Ask" *enCourage* (blog), July 2, 2018, https://encourage.pcacdm.org/2018/07/02/post-template-43/.

"She continued to hope and pray for change, but she could do little else. After all, what could one woman do to change a great society?"

—Fannie Lou Hamer[6]

Name/Date	Prayer Request

[6] Quoted by David Rubel. *Fannie Lou Hamer: From Sharecropping to Politics.* (Englewood Cliffs, NJ: Silver Burdette Press, 1990), 45.

"Some people think going to God with the small things in our lives belittles him, making him small in our own eyes. This is true if we only ever go to him with our own wants and needs. But our heavenly Father is big enough to handle both requests for his kingdom to come and for our daily bread. He is powerful enough to shoulder our troubles and the burdens of the rest of the world day in and day out."

—Faith Chang[7]

Name/Date	Prayer Request

[7] Faith Chang, "Those Common, Hard Things." *Reformed Margins* (blog), November 14, 2019, https://reformedmargins.com/common-hard-things/ .

"When the difficulties of life mute us, remember it is not how well we pray, but that we pray."
—Christina Fox[8]

Name/Date	Prayer Request

[8] Christina Fox, "God Hears Your Wordless Prayers." *Christina Fox* (blog), January 26, 2021, https://www.christinafox.com/blog/2020/12/24/god-hears-your-wordless-prayers).

> "Faith does not eliminate questions. But faith knows where to take them."
>
> —Elisabeth Elliot[9]

Name/Date	Prayer Request

---

[9] Elisabeth Elliot, *A Chance to Die: The Life and Legacy of Amy Carmichael* (Old Tappan, NJ: F.H. Revell Co., 1987), 55.

"Bask in this truth heading into whatever lies ahead, knowing that if you are in Christ, your name is on his lips right now."
—Sue Harris[10]

Name/Date	Prayer Request

---

[10] Sue Harris, "Our Savior's Moment by Moment Intercession." *enCourage* (blog), March 29, 2021, https://encourage.pcacdm.org/2021/03/29/post-template-213-119/.

> "One of the kindest, servant-hearted things someone can do is to pray for another person."
> —Melissa B. Kruger[11]

Name/Date	Prayer Request

---

[11] Hunter Beless, "Joy: Interview with Melissa Kruger," *Journeywomen* (podcast audio), June 4, 2018, https://journeywomenpodcast.com/episode/ep-54-joy.

Suggested Discussion Questions for Small Groups

These are suggestions for discussing the lesson in a group of women after reading the chapter and watching the video lesson or listening to the podcast (www.pcacdm.org/messy). The first question is italicized because it is an icebreaker with the following ones as discussion prompts. You may also open up the time by asking if anyone has a question from the book they would like to bring to the group. Don't forget to lead the group in prayer, asking for God's wisdom and kind conversation.

Chapter One
The Not So Fabulous Five

1. *What is the worst mess you have ever had to clean up?*
2. How do you react to the catechism definition of sin?
3. Let's discuss ways women's lives can be messy due to sin (ours, others', the brokenness of our world).
4. Were you surprised by the women Matthew includes in his introduction of Jesus in Matthew 1. Why?
5. Why did Jesus have to be a human living in our messy world to save us?
6. What is comforting to you in your story about how God treated these ladies in their stories?

Chapter Two
God's Story

1. *What's the scariest thing you've ever done?*
2. Let's review the covenants discussed in this chapter. Do you have any questions about how the concept of covenant impacts your relationship with God?
3. How do you think God felt about Adam and Eve's first sin?
4. Describe how salvation is a gift from God. How does this grace ("free gift") make you feel?

5. Name some ways you have seen God impact others by working in your individual story.
6. If God is using your story as He weaves His Big Story, how do you feel about
   a. The purpose of your life?
   b. How others' lives intersect with yours?
   c. How to pray?

Chapter Three
The Desperate Daughter-in-Law

1. *What is the most vulnerable you have ever felt (this can be funny or serious)?*
2. What are ways women today find themselves vulnerable like Tamar was?
3. Do you think Tamar imagined how special her (oldest) baby would be? What are examples of God doing more than you imagine in your difficult circumstances?
4. Judah neglected to obey the law God put into place to protect the needy like Tamar. How do Christians today not obey God's laws when it comes to protecting the vulnerable in our society?
5. Why did Judah not want to give his third son to Tamar? Name reasons we tend to ignore needs around us.
6. How do we know Judah repented?
7. If someone repents of neglecting you, how do you find the strength to forgive?

Chapter Four
The Career Prostitute

1. *Share a story of your sweating out a risky decision.*
2. Rahab risked her life to hide the spies. Why? How?
3. Name things women have to risk to follow God today.
4. Were you disturbed about the fall of Jericho?
   a. What does the total destruction teach us about God?
   b. What does the saving of Rahab and her family teach us about God?

Suggested Discussion Questions

5. How can you make your church and community make women with a sinful past feel welcome?

Chapter Five
The Ultimate Outsider

1. *Name a moment when you walked into the room and felt like a total outsider.*
2. Where do women go for financial and emotional stability? Where do you tend to go?
3. Why did Naomi go towards God and His people when God let all those bad things happen to her family? Do you ever feel tempted to run from, rather than towards, God and His people?
4. Name circumstances when you felt overwhelmed or bitter like Naomi.
5. What can God's people do to help women who are bitter, overwhelmed, or "outsiders"?
6. How can you practice going toward God instead of other people or possessions for security?

Chapter Six
From Ultimate Outsider to Ultimate Insider

1. *Name a person you would call a hero or heroine in your life.*
2. Who is the hero of Ruth and Naomi's story? How does he provide a pattern of Jesus, our Redeemer?
3. God is obviously in charge of Ruth's story. How do you feel about His being in charge of yours? Is that comforting or irritating?
4. Name some ways God provides for you through others' keeping His commands.
5. Discuss ways you as an individual and as a community of believers can provide for others' needs.
6. What are some ways you feel needy today? Recount times God gave you protection "under His wings."

Chapter Seven
The Queen of Messy

1. *Have you ever experienced a good ending to an unhappy story?*
2. How would you have felt in Bathsheba's shoes?
3. How does God define sin? How does our society define sin? How do you define sin?
4. Whether sinner or sinned against, how do sexual sins impact a woman's identity today?
5. How should we learn from David's repentance and God's forgiveness and restoration of this family?
6. What does it mean that Matthew included Bathsheba as "the wife of Uriah the Hittite" in his genealogy? Name ways our community can be intentional to include women with a complicated past.

Chapter Eight
The Unwed Teen Mother

1. *Name a time you felt like you were misunderstood because of your age.*
2. Contrast the reactions to Gabriel by Zechariah and Mary. Describe times in your life when God's Word did not make sense.
3. Name some impossible things God is asking you to believe today.
4. Why do you think the gospel writers connected all the prophecies to Mary's Child? How does that impact how you view God's power over His Big Story of redemption?
5. When your plans get changed, big or little ones, how do you respond? How can knowing God's character help you respond well?
6. Some people believe that good things happen to good people. How does Mary's story—and Jesus's life and death—contradict that idea?

Suggested Discussion Questions

Chapter Nine
Magnificat!

1. *What is your favorite song? When are you most likely to sing out loud?*
2. Recount some things Mary sang about God. Do any resonate with your view of God today?
3. How does the fact that God rejoices over you with singing make you feel?
4. Can you name big ways God moved using small or messy things in your life?
5. Why do you think Mary went to see Elizabeth? Describe a time when God used another woman to encourage your faith in God.
6. What is one thing you learned from this study? How will you incorporate that into your life?